Early Childhood Education in Aotearoa New Zealand

Critical Cultural Studies of Childhood
Series Editors: **Marianne N. Bloch, Gaile Sloan Cannella,** and **Beth Blue Swadener**

This series focuses on reframings of theory, research, policy, and pedagogies in childhood. A critical cultural study of childhood is one that offers a "prism" of possibilities for writing about power and its relationship to the cultural constructions of childhood, family, and education in broad societal, local, and global contexts. Books in the series open up new spaces for dialogue and reconceptualization based on critical theoretical and methodological framings, including critical pedagogy; advocacy and social justice perspectives; cultural, historical, and comparative studies of childhood; and post-structural, postcolonial, and/or feminist studies of childhood, family, and education. The intent of the series is to examine the relations between power, language, and what is taken as normal/abnormal, good, and natural, to understand the construction of the "other," difference and inclusions/exclusions that are embedded in current notions of childhood, family, educational reforms, policies, and the practices of schooling. *Critical Cultural Studies of Childhood* will open up dialogue about new possibilities for action and research.

Single-authored as well as edited volumes focusing on critical studies of childhood from a variety of disciplinary and theoretical perspectives are included in the series. A particular focus is in a reimagining and critical reflection on policy and practice in early childhood, primary, and elementary education. The series intends to open up new spaces for reconceptualizing theories and traditions of research, policies, cultural reasonings, and practices at all of these levels, in the United States, as well as comparatively.

Titles include:

Jenny Ritchie and Mere Skerrett
EARLY CHILDHOOD EDUCATION IN AOTEAROA NEW ZEALAND
History, Pedagogy, and Liberation

Marianne N. Bloch, Devorah Kennedy, Theodora Lightfoot, and Dar Weyenberg (*editors*);
Foreword by Thomas S. Popkewitz
THE CHILD IN THE WORLD/THE WORLD IN THE CHILD
Education and the Configuration of a Universal, Modern, and Globalized Childhood

Soula Mitakidou, Evangelia Tressou, Beth Blue Swadener, and Carl A. Grant (*editors*)
BEYOND PEDAGOGIES OF EXCLUSION IN DIVERSE CHILDHOOD CONTEXTS
Transnational Challenges

Glenda Mac Naughton and Karina Davis (*editors*)
"RACE" AND EARLY CHILDHOOD EDUCATION
An International Approach to Identity, Politics, and Pedagogy

Majia Holmer Nadesan
GOVERNING CHILDHOOD INTO THE 21ST CENTURY
Biopolitical Technologies of Childhood Management and Education

Kyunghwa Lee and Mark D. Vagle (*editors*)
DEVELOPMENTALISM IN EARLY CHILDHOOD AND MIDDLE GRADES EDUCATION
Critical Conversations on Readiness and Responsiveness

Hillel Goelman, Jayne Pivik, and Martin Guhn (*editors*)
NEW APPROACHES TO EARLY CHILD DEVELOPMENT
Rules, Rituals, and Realities

Judith Duncan and Sarah Te One (*editors*)
COMPARATIVE EARLY CHILDHOOD EDUCATION SERVICES
International Perspectives

palgrave▶pivot

Early Childhood Education in Aotearoa New Zealand: History, Pedagogy, and Liberation

Jenny Ritchie
Associate Professor, Early Childhood Education, Unitec Institute of Technology, New Zealand

and

Mere Skerrett
Senior Lecturer, School of Teacher Education, University of Canterbury, New Zealand

palgrave
macmillan

EARLY CHILDHOOD EDUCATION IN AOTEAROA NEW ZEALAND
Copyright © Jenny Ritchie and Mere Skerrett, 2014.
Foreword © Marianne N. Bloch, 2014.

All rights reserved.

First published in 2014 by
PALGRAVE MACMILLAN®
in the United States—a division of St. Martin's Press LLC,
175 Fifth Avenue, New York, NY 10010.

Where this book is distributed in the UK, Europe and the rest of the world, this is by Palgrave Macmillan, a division of Macmillan Publishers Limited, registered in England, company number 785998, of Houndmills, Basingstoke, Hampshire RG21 6XS.

Palgrave Macmillan is the global academic imprint of the above companies and has companies and representatives throughout the world.

Palgrave® and Macmillan® are registered trademarks in the United States, the United Kingdom, Europe and other countries.

ISBN: 978–1–137–37580–3   EPUB
ISBN: 978–1–137–37579–7   PDF
ISBN: 978–1–137–39441–5   Hardback

Library of Congress Cataloging-in-Publication Data is available from the Library of Congress.

A catalogue record of the book is available from the British Library.

First edition: 2014

www.palgrave.com/pivot

DOI: 10.1057/9781137375797

Contents

Foreword by Marianne N. Bloch ix

Series Editors' Preface xiv

Te Timatanga: Introduction and Overview 1
Jenny Ritchie and Mere Skerrett
    Part A: Chapters 1–3 (Mere Skerrett) 4
    Part B: Chapters 4–6 (Jenny Ritchie) 5
    References 7

Part A   Kaupapa Māori Early Childhood Care and Education

1 Dismantling Colonial Myths: Centralising Māori Language in Education 10
Mere Skerrett
    Introduction 11
    Colonization and homogenization in education 12
    Power hierarchies through geographic territorialization and sociolinguistic stratification 13
    Linguafaction 17
    Discourse analysis 18
    Powerful discourses and society 18
    Myth one: we are all (happy) New Zealanders: trick or treaty 20
    Myth two: colonization is benevolent; therefore Māori ungrateful 24

Myth three: what? racism in New Zealand, never! 27
  Conclusions 29
  Notes 31
  References 32

2 Policy and Inhibiters of Bicultural/Bilingual Advancement 35
  Mere Skerrett

  Introduction 36
  The 1835 Declaration of Independence and 1840
    Te Tiriti o Waitangi 37
  The Treaty of Waitangi and the 1987 Lands Case 40
  The Māori Language Act 41
  The Treaty in Education 42
  The rise and decline of Kōhanga Reo 43
  Policy documents—The Meade report 44
  Before Five policy statement 44
  Pathways to the Future 45
  The impact of *Pathways* policy on
    bilingual/immersion settings 46
  Ka Hikitia Māori education strategies and
    Tau Mai Te Reo 47
  Conclusions 51
  Notes 53
  References 53

3 Crown Breaches, Neoliberal Reforms, and
  Radical Pedagogy 56
  Mere Skerrett

  Introduction 57
  Waitangi Tribunal reports 58
  Funding inequities 58
  Declining enrollments for Kōhanga Reo 59
  Tribunal findings of Crown Treaty breaches 60
  Curriculum implications 60
  Teacher education 61
  Regulatory framework 62
  Neoliberal reforms 63
  Radical (critical) Kaupapa Māori pedagogy 66
  The development of critical literacy 68
  Conclusions 68

Notes		70
References		70

Part B Indigenizing "Whitestream" Early Childhood Care and Education Practice in Aotearoa

4 Contextual Explorations of Māori within "Whitestream" Early Childhood Education in Aotearoa New Zealand   73
Jenny Ritchie

- Introduction   74
- Promises, promises: *Te Tiriti* and *Te Whāriki* as ethical visions   75
- Settler assumption of sovereignty   75
- Progressive traditions   77
- "Flax-roots" early childhood education and care services   78
- Māori pre-schools   79
- Chance to be equal   81
- Repositioning te Ao Māori as central to education   83
- New right enmeshment with liberal social policies   85
- Note   87
- References   87

5 Post-*Te Whāriki* Early Childhood Care and Education Policy and Practice in "Whitestream" Early Childhood Care and Education in Aotearoa   92
Jenny Ritchie

- Background   93
- Neoliberal discursive era   94
- *Te Whāriki* as a kaupapa Māori vision   97
- Ministry of Education guidance   100
- Reviewing implementation   104
- Attaining and maintaining momentum   105
- Note   106
- References   107

6 A Counter-Colonial Pedagogy of Affect in Early Childhood Education in Aotearoa New Zealand   113
Jenny Ritchie

- Background   114

Data examples	117
Conclusion	125
Note	125
References	126
Liberatory Praxis: Conclusions	**130**
Mere Skerrett and Jenny Ritchie	
Colonization and Linguafaction	131
Systemic change	131
Māori language narratives	133
Māori language narratives as curriculum	133
Shifting the "whitestream"	134
References	137
Index	**139**

Foreword

I should begin by saying that, as one of the two series editors for the Palgrave Macmillan series "Critical Cultural Studies of Childhood" (with Beth Blue Swadener), we solicited this book because we felt it might provide an example of ways in which early childhood and pre-school pedagogical and policy practices might be challenged in the USA, as well as elsewhere. I was interested in this particular story because of my professional admiration for the specific authors' work, and their work with many others requiring long-term activism (legal, social, cultural, political, economic). These educational, legal, and cultural scholars/pedagogical experts/activists claimed something fairly simple, but so very hard to achieve: a legal and legitimized space for pre-schools and schools that would acknowledge, respect, and honor a community's or a nation's cultural and linguistic "heritage of knowledge" as critical to maintain, augment, represent, elaborate, and cherish. The work of Jenny Ritchie, Mere Skerrett, and others who helped in the development, promotion, and elaboration, and critique of *Te Whāriki: He whāriki mātauranga mō ngā mokopuna o Aotearoa: Early childhood curriculum* (Ministry of Education, 1996) in Aotearoa, New Zealand offers an illustration of what might be considered as "high-quality" curriculum and pedagogical practices even in a time of continuing colonial and assimilative educational practices, and a global discourse that highlights the individual (child, parent, national competitiveness) over the collective caring for a society, for children, for families, and for the honoring and maintenance of cultural and linguistic knowledge. In many parts of the world, global discourses of competition, individualism, the private over the public, the need for personal (rather than collective) "responsibility," and high "standards" for "all children" has taken hold (Bloch, Kennedy, Lightfoot, & Weyenberg, 2006; Fuller, 2007). Quality is measured similarly across preschool and school sites in order to achieve the global high achieving "standard" child; "no child left behind" typically suggests that there are certain children (and families or groups) that are behind, and need intervention to become standard (read this as "normal"). But in an attempt to universalize younger and older children, to standardize them, whose *standards* are privileged? Whose knowledge is acknowledged as most important/less important? In the case of the Māori, a majority-minority group in New Zealand, a former British colony, we have an *unusual* case where acknowledgment of the legal right to build a curriculum around Māori culture and language followed commitments made in the Treaty of Waitangi, giving legal precedent for the development and maintenance of a curriculum that honors Māori knowledge and language (Ritchie & Rau, 2010), while also fitting into national and global standards for the schooling/education of all citizens. This case is unusual because the legal Treaty included acknowledgment of these rights, and financial support to build preschool and school curriculum, and to run programs that embodied the principles of collectivity, respect for community members, cultural and linguistic rights, and indigenous knowledge—as well as "knowledge" that would be valued and valuable to all as New Zealand citizens, British citizens, and global citizens. The stories these chapters tell are historical, and specific, setting the stage for the special case of Māori education within the New Zealand context. But they are also more general. They speak to the effort to make a curriculum, to train teachers, to involve a community in restoring languages that were virtually "lost," or, as the authors suggest, a linguacide (the killing of yet another indigenous language) through assimilation, and colonization—of language and cultural knowledge. They speak to the efforts it has taken to build a culturally relevant, linguistically rich bilingual/bicultural curriculum for young children—when there are few remaining speakers of Māori. They speak of success, and, of continuing struggles, in the face of continuing discourses of universalization, individualization of responsibility, and of the importance of "standardized" children and knowledge.But what makes this book unique, I believe, is the recording of the history of resistance, territorialization, and deterritorialization; we see unusual successes within the New Zealand context where indigenous Māori researchers, legal experts, sociologists, critical cultural studies experts, politicians, and educators have worked together to overcome obstacles that few other countries or groups have been able to overcome. Drawing on their own work, their elders' work, and the work of, for example, Frantz Fanon, L. T. Smith (1999), Paulo Freire, Michel Foucault, Gilles Deleuze, and Felix Guattari, they suggest the power to examine "whose knowledge counts" is both local, and global, and that the fight is ongoing, unpredictable, but moving—geographically and culturally stratified—but with spaces for new ideas, and promising inventions. They highlight the continual "reterritorialization" of efforts to create pedagogical practices that honor and create a blend of traditional indigenous knowledge with ever-changing "new" ways of being/knowing. They highlight current challenges of reterritorialization by the increasing globalized standards and assessments "for all" movements that are swirling across nations. But, in the same way, their book illustrates the specificity of the Māori/New Zealand context, and the legal rights to contest a standardized assimilational (and deficit-oriented) approach to education; their work shows ways to move beyond, between, and around in continuing efforts to rebuild the Māori language, even in the face of few teachers, and few adults who know Māori; they illustrate their efforts to assess the curriculum in ways that respect what the community hopes children will learn, rather than simply what the global community has determined, for the moment, are standards of high-quality learning and outcomes.In writing this story, there are no ways to ignore the difficulties they outline that were faced in the past, and those being faced in the present, in what had been a shining story of cultural and language maintenance, and creativity in preschool education, and in curriculum development more generally. Around the world, however, these pressures are being faced—often in less hospitable, less ethical environments, and with fewer legal rights. The evidence honors what they are doing, and tells us of dangers in doing otherwise (see, for example, Soto, 2010; Tochon, 2009).I am reminded sometimes of a story from a Madison, Wisconsin school policy in the early 2000s—which failed to make sense to me then, but seems pertinent now. The schools were, at that time, moving children whose primary home languages were Hmong and Spanish into English Language Learning (ELL) classroom environments, as fast as possible, in order to help fabricate "minority language learners" as excellent English learners as fast as possible, to help their early school learning. At the same time, the policies were suggesting that all high school and university students, in order to be prepared for an increasingly competitive global cultural and economic environment, should study about "other cultures" and learn at least one other language with proficiency. Study abroad experiences were initiated; international/global education schools were formed as optional private experiences open typically to wealthier students. Why, I asked then and now, would we engage in policies that kill languages and cultural knowledge in the early years, while trying to promote them in middle, high, and university education? While there is somewhat greater acceptance of the value of bilingual/bicultural immersion schools now than a decade ago, these are often framed from a deficiency model approach (let's catch them early, try to maintain "their" language and customs, while fast tracking "our" language and customs), or they are available to an affluent few, even those involved in "parental choices." Why kill languages and cultural knowledge in the early or later years (Soto, 2010; Tochon, 2009)? Why not honor and maintain a cultural complexity that is representative of the world cultures and languages that exist? How can we imagine each child and their parents and communities as "rich" and "competent" and creative, as filled with knowledge to share, rather than as always "lacking?" As Deleuze and Guattari (1987) and others suggest, the concept of the "lacking child" can so easily be moved into one that acknowledges the strengths, ideas, and creativity of even the smallest and youngest amongst us. We can honor our collective and diverse ideas, knowledge systems, and the intersectionality of language/culture, rather than begin anew—for a few—in later years. Do we want a standard child, with standard ways of assessment of child, parent, program, and teacher, or do we want to entertain new ways of imagining what richness and diversity of knowledge we already have in our schools and communities? How can this story, in this book about one internationally known experimental curriculum, suggest other ways of thinking about our communities as collectives, as ones in which we care about all children, their families, and an ethical way of honoring interests, competence, and knowledge? The discourses of individual success, competition, personal responsibility, and the private over the public—while prevalent—are not always those that need to be privileged. We can do things quite differently, and it isn't too late. While in New Zealand, legal rights to an education that promotes a different way of knowing, different outcomes that can be privileged as important give hope to those who are still fighting—including the authors of this book. In the USA and elsewhere, the rights of all children to understand the richness of all children's knowledge systems should be upheld; the human/children's right to maintain one's rich language/cultural customs should be acknowledged. Killing languages and customs as part of a continuing attempt to assimilate, colonize, or demean diverse and complex and rich communities should not be continued. Difficult to do, you might say. Read this book, and you can see how this fight can be argued, envisioned, and implemented.

Marianne N. Bloch
University of Wisconsin-Madison

References

Bloch, M. N., Kennedy, D., Lightfoot, T., & Weyenberg, D. (Eds) (2006). *The Child in the World/The World in the Child: Education and the Configuration of a Universal, Modern, and Globalized Child.* New York: Palgrave Macmillan.

Deleuze, G., & Guattari, F. (1987). *A Thousand Plateaus: Capitalism and Schizophrenia.* Minneapolis: University of Minnesota Press.

Fuller, B. (2007). *Standardized Childhood: The Political and Cultural Struggle Over Early Education.* Palo Alto, CA: Stanford University Press.

Ritchie, J., & Rau, C. (2010). Kia mau ki te wairuatanga. Countercolonial narratives of early childhood education in Aotearoa. In G. S. Cannella, & L. D. Soto (Eds). *Childhoods: A Handbook* (pp. 355–373). New York: Peter Lang.

Smith, L. T. (1999). *Decolonizing Methodologies: Research and Indigenous Peoples.* London: Zed Books.

Soto, L. D. (2010). Diversity, linguistics, and the silencing of social justice. In G. S. Cannella, & L. D. Soto (Eds), *Childhoods: A Handbook* (pp. 215–230). New York: Peter Lang.

Tochon, F. V. (2009). The key to global understanding: World language education—why schools need to adapt. *Review of Educational Research, 79*(2), 650–681.

Series Editors' Preface

We enthusiastically welcome this volume to the Critical Cultural Studies of Childhood Studies series, as it embodies our intentions for the series in multiple and nuanced ways. In their examination of dynamics of power, language, and culture as embedded in the colonization of Indigenous (Māori) childhoods in Aotearoa New Zealand, as well as framing possibilities for emancipation, Jenny Ritchie and Mere Skerrett confront the racism and linguicide and linguafaction embodied in colonial relations and offer Māori language narratives and a counter-colonial pedagogy for early childhood education in Aotearoa. Long recognized for innovative curricula and culturally grounded approaches to early years' care and learning, notably the *Te Whāriki: He whāriki mātauranga mō ngā mokopuna o Aotearoa: Early childhood curriculum* (Ministry of Education, 1996) and other early childhood initiatives, Aotearoa offers both a contested space of persistent colonial education patterns and of powerful interruptions and reclaiming projects.

This volume reflects the cumulative and combined scholarship of some of the most respected reconceptualist early childhood scholars in Aotearoa New Zealand and internationally. It also draws from extensive culturally grounded and critical studies of early childhood that focus not only on the promise and practice of *Te Whāriki*, but on the decrease in Māori language speakers in early childhood programs and other "whitestream" issues in the sector. Confronting the need to strengthen the bicultural/bilingual competencies of early educators, the authors make a strong case for reaffirming Māori values and resisting neoliberalism and its emphasis on individualism. In their call for resistance to Western-dominated pedagogies and for a deepened respect for Indigenous cultural values, the authors confront both the barriers to and possibilities of early childhood programs, curricula, pedagogies, and interactions with families to offer a space of cultural reaffirmation and counter colonial research and practices that will resonate with other postcolonial contexts worldwide.

Beth Blue Swadener and Marianne N. Bloch

palgrave▸pivot

www.palgrave.com/pivot

Te Timatanga: Introduction and Overview

Jenny Ritchie and Mere Skerrett

Ritchie J., and M. Skerrett. *Early Childhood Education in Aotearoa New Zealand: History, Pedagogy, and Liberation.* New York: Palgrave Macmillan, 2014.
DOI: 10.1057/9781137375797.0004.

The milieu of early childhood care and education in Aotearoa New Zealand is acknowledged internationally for several reasons. One aspect that is unusual within the international context is the recognition given to the Indigenous Māori within the New Zealand early childhood curriculum, *"Te Whāriki: He whāriki mātauranga mō ngā mokopuna o Aotearoa"* (New Zealand Ministry of Education, 1996), along with a stated commitment to Te Tiriti o Waitangi/The Treaty of Waitangi of 1840, a founding document of the nation (Ritchie & Rau, 2006). Secondly, *Te Whāriki* has been recognized for its sociocultural and integrated nature (Nuttall, 2003; Ritchie & Buzzelli, 2012). Thirdly, the document has at its heart a set of principles that focus on the centrality of relationships within early childhood care and education; the empowerment of young children and their families; recognizing the ecologies of families and communities; and the holistic way that young children learn. This book seeks to demonstrate some of the contributions and dilemmas that have arisen in the field of early childhood care and education in Aotearoa New Zealand in relation to these aspects (Skerrett, 2001, 2003, 2010, 2013; Ritchie, 2003, 2012).

In elucidating the specific context of early childhood care and education in Aotearoa, with a particular emphasis on the ways in which the recent policy context has operated in an attempt to effect inclusion of Māori epistemologies and pedagogies within both Māori initiatives such as Te Kōhanga Reo (a Māori immersion *whānau*/family development movement), as well as "mainstream" institutions, this book offers insight into struggles to provide culturally equitable provision to Indigenous young children.

The colonization of Aotearoa New Zealand by Great Britain began in the early 1800s, much later in the colonization chronology than most other countries. This was an international era of "ideological ferment," contextualized by "the rise of science, [and] the French, American and Industrial revolutions" (Belich, 2009, p. 163). By the mid-1830s, the tide had begun turning, internationally, against slavery, as human rights discourses began to gain traction. These discourses were unfavorably received by those benefitting from the colonialist economic booms that were sustained through slave labor (Belich, 2009). Britain abolished slavery between 1834 and 1838, and these discourses were influential in the British Colonial Office during the same period (Moon, 2002). All of the land within the islands of Aotearoa were acknowledged by the Colonial Office to be held by the various Māori tribes, as seen in the phrase "Ko te kingitanga, ko te mana i te whenua" (the kingship and power of the land), as residing with the Chiefs (Walker, 2004, p. 88). In

1835, northern Māori chiefs, under the guidance of James Busby, who had an official title as "British Resident" prepared and signed a Declaration of Independence, in which they stated that "All sovereign power and authority within [their] territories ... [was] declared to reside entirely and exclusively in their collective capacity" (as cited in Walker, 2004, p. 88). British settlers continued to flow into the country, and by the end of 1939, the Colonial Office deemed it necessary to legitimate this de facto colonization. Captain William Hobson was despatched to New Zealand to secure a treaty that would formalize this. The instructions given to Hobson by Lord Normanby of the Colonial Office acknowledged New Zealand as a sovereign state (under Māori leadership) and counselled Hobson to ensure that his treaty-making process acknowledged "the free and intelligent consent" of the Natives (Walker, 2004, p. 90).

In the Māori version of Te Tiriti o Waitangi, Māori ceded governance (*kawanatanga*) to the British Crown (Article One), whilst retaining their absolute chieftainship (*tino rangatiratanga*) over their lands, villages, and everything of value (Article Two). Māori were also to be considered equal to British citizens (Article Three) and in a fourth protocol read to the assembled Chiefs at the initial treaty signing at Waitangi, Māori belief systems were to be considered as equal to the state religions of Britain and France (Orange, 1987). Through these agreements, Māori expected that their *mana* (power, authority) would be upheld in future transactions with the British Crown. Unfortunately, the ethical aspirations of Articles Two and Three of Te Tiriti o Waitangi were buried under the onslaught of settlerism (Belich, 2009), facilitated when in 1852 the settlers obtained rule of the country as independent from Britain. In transporting the British Westminster parliamentary system to New Zealand, Māori were excluded from the franchise (as Māori did not have land title as individuals, since their lands were collectively owned). Māori scholar Ranginui Walker has critiqued this "institutionalisation of racism at the inception of democracy in New Zealand" (Walker, 2004, p. 111).

This major, fundamental exclusion has had long-standing impacts on Māori. Even though later (1867) changes provided voting rights to initially those Māori men who had by then obtained individual titles, the potential Māori electoral impact was constrained to the selection of only four Māori seats in parliament. Māori quickly became a minority within their own country, and the majoritarian parliamentary system denied them a strong voice for many years. By around 1900 the Māori population had been decimated, and Māori were referred to as a "dying race" (Te Rangi

Hiroa (P. H. Buck), 1924). Māori nonetheless maintained an ongoing struggle to have their understandings of treaty rights acknowledged and to be granted restitution for breaches. These breaches resulted in large-scale land loss, prohibition of cultural practices, and the near-obliteration of Māori language(s) that were also perceived to be "dying" by the 1970s, when only 5 per cent of Māori still spoke their own language (Waitangi Tribunal, 1986). These historical colonial impositions have left an ongoing legacy of resentment and anger, and thus need to be foregrounded in any discussion of contemporary education in Aotearoa New Zealand.

Languages encapsulate cultures, values, histories, traditions, stories, and ways of knowing, being, and doing. The Māori language remains under threat. A recent report by the Waitangi Tribunal, a government-established commission that examines Māori claims of Treaty/Tiriti breaches, stated that:

> We find te reo Māori to be approaching a state of crisis. In census, preschool, and school statistics there are diminishing proportions and, in many cases, numbers of te reo speakers and learners. Older native speakers passing away are simply not being replaced. Having begun a process of revitalisation in the late 1970s, it seems that te reo is now in renewed and steady decline. (Waitangi Tribunal, 2011, p. 708)

This book is divided into two sections, each of three chapters. In writing separately/together we were aware that our work represented a rhizomatic assemblage comprising "circles of convergence" (Deleuze & Guattari, 2004, p. 24) and we also deliberately intended that each chapter would stand alone.

Part A: Chapters 1–3 (Mere Skerrett)

Chapter 1 traverses the colonial context and offers a discourse analysis (Foucault, 1972), exploring some of the influences shaping colonial thinking that remain alive and well in the dominion of Aotearoa/New Zealand. Implicit in Deleuze and Guattari's (2004) notion of deterritorialization is the restructuring of a place or territory that has experienced harmful territorialization through patriarchal hierarchies of colonization. Unmasking the power hierarchies (Cannella, 2011) of colonization serves to dismantle them, to dehegemonize them. Counter-colonial readings of texts allow for alternative interpretations of the spaces we occupy, suggesting alternative discourses. The discourse analysis in this chapter is designed to unsettle settler historiographies in Aotearoa/New Zealand and challenge the one-sided partnerships that developed through the Courts as they undermined the founding documents that allowed for British settlement: the 1835 Declaration of Independence and the 1840 Treaty of Waitangi. It is argued that the re-generation of *te reo* Māori (the Māori language) is transformative in that it repositions Māori knowledge/s and language/s at the core of curriculum and the centre of communities. Drawing on Freirian concepts of transformative praxis (Freire, 1972), the revernacularization of the Māori language resists archaic teaching pedagogies and practices, dismantles fixed truths, challenges knowledge monopolies, and troubles the hierarchical power structures that are endemic in the colonial state. The concept of "linguafaction," coined by the author of this section (language eradication, land alienation, and culture shock due to colonization), is introduced and it is asserted that through exposing the harmful effects of linguafaction, the system can be, and is being, dehegemonized. Chapters 2 and 3 provide overviews of the policy environment that inhibits the bilingual/bicultural advancement of Aotearoa/New Zealand with a deeper analysis of the Waitangi Tribunal Reports of 2010 and 2012, with regard to the Treaty breaches in education (Waitangi Tribunal, 2010, 2012). Counter-colonial discourses through renarrativization provide the critique required in order to dehegemonize the system. This section shows how the success of Kōhanga Reo and the whole of the Māori medium sector is indeed a powerful force for reshaping the system that is still currently lagging behind the practice. The incorporation of *te reo* Māori (Māori language) fully into the core curriculum is the next step up for the education system.

Part B: Chapters 4–6 (Jenny Ritchie)

Part B of the book revolves around the consideration that both *Te Tiriti o Waitangi* and *Te Whāriki* are foundational documents, holding an ethical vision of hope for co-habitation of Tangata Whenua (people of the land—Indigenous people) and *Tangata Tiriti* (people who now live in Aotearoa as a result of the Tiriti o Waitangi agreement that allowed for settlement by Britain) (Bell, 2006; Grace, 2000; Williams, 2004). Chapter 4 provides a perspective on the history of Māori as they encountered early childhood care and education offerings within the assemblage(s) of the colonization project. Instead of a view of Māori as static victims of British colonization, Māori are seen as active agents within the assemblage(s), generating and maximizing potentialities in response to the territorialization of settlerism and capitalism. Egalitarian, social justice ethics were undoubtedly present, but often sabotaged by majoritarianism and the shear deluge of Anglo/white settlement. The Māori population quickly reduced from being the sole sovereign inhabitants of their lands pre-Anglo settlement, to a population equal to that of the settlers within 18 years of Te Tiriti/The Treaty having been signed, and by 1890, they had become less than 10 per cent of the total population in their own country (Belich, 2009).

Chapter 4 proceeds to outline the origins of the various "flaxroots," early childhood movements including Māori preschools of the 1960s and the "compensatory" Te Kohanga Preschool Project of the 1970s. It then overviews the initial introduction of The Treaty of Waitangi into official early childhood education discourse in the Labour government policy document "Before Five" of 1988, and concludes by introducing the era of neoliberalism in Aotearoa New Zealand.

Chapter 5, after a brief contextualizing background section, locates the writing of *Te Whāriki* within an era of increasing neoliberalist social and economic policy, whereby the economics of privatization, individualism, and competition began to usurp the remaining threads of an egalitarian, collectivist ethic within social policy. *Te Whāriki* is positioned internationally as unique in being a curriculum grounded in Indigenous onto-epistemology in which *kaupapa* Māori (Māori philosophy) supports an envisioning of social justice praxis. The *kaupapa* Māori frame is viewed as providing a coherent organizing framework, allowing integration of a range of theories, including sociocultural theory, alongside cognitivist oriented developmental psychology and constructivism. *Te Whāriki* is also strongly holistic, and *whānau*/family centred, allowing for shared generation of narratives via responsive and reciprocal relationships inclusive of the voices of *tamariki* (children) and parents/*whānau*. The chapter then moves on to an advisedly selective overview of a range of documents. It points that out that recent government-facilitated reviews of practice show that educator enactment of the "bicultural" aspirations of *Te Whāriki* has been disappointing, and highlights teacher education as a potential site for transformation in this process toward realizing the vision of *Te Whāriki*.

Chapter 6 draws upon some data from three recent studies that purposively focussed on implementation of *Te Whāriki* by teachers committed to enactment in alignment with *Te Tiriti o Waitangi* obligations to respectfully engage with *whānau* Māori and reflect *te ao* Māori onto-epistemologies, suggesting that this might constitute a "pedagogy of affect" reflecting deep openness and responsiveness to children and families.

References

Belich, J. (2009). *Replenishing the Earth: The Settler Revolution and the Rise of the Anglo-world, 1783–1939*. Oxford: Oxford University Press.

Bell, A. (2006). Bifurcation or entanglement? Settler identity and biculturalism in Aotearoa New Zealand. *Continuum: Journal of Media & Culture Studies, 20*(2), 253–268.

Cannella, G. S. (2011). Political possibility, hypercapitalism, and the "conservative reeducation machine." *Cultural Studies ↔ Critical Methodologies, 11*(4), 364–368.

Deleuze, G., & Guattari, F. (2004). *A Thousand Plateaus. Capitalism and Schizophrenia* (B. Massumi, Trans.). London and New York: Continuum.

Foucault, M. (1972). *The Archaeology of Knowledge* (A. M. S. Smith, Trans.). London: Routledge.

Freire, P. (1972). *Pedagogy of the Oppressed*. London: Penguin.

Grace, P. (2000). *The Treaty of Waitangi and the Expression of Culture in Aotearoa*. Tamaki Makaurau/Auckland.

Moon, P. (2002). *Te Ara Kī Te Tiriti: The Path to the Treaty of Waitangi*. Auckland: David Ling.

New Zealand Ministry of Education. (1996). *Te Whāriki. He whāriki mātauranga mō ngā mokopuna o Aotearoa: Early Childhood Curriculum*. Wellington: Learning Media. Retrieved from http://www.educate.ece.govt.nz/~/media/Educate/Files/Reference%20Downloads/whariki.pdf

Nuttall, J. (2003). Introduction. In J. Nuttall (Ed.), *Weaving Te Whāriki: Aotearoa New Zealand's Early Childhood Curriculum Document in Theory and Practice* (pp. 5–15). Wellington: New Zealand Council for Educational Research.

Orange, C. (1987). *The Treaty of Waitangi*. Wellington: Allen and Unwin/Port Nicholson Press.

Ritchie, J., & Rau, C. (2006). *Whakawhanaungatanga. Partnerships in bicultural development in early childhood education*. Final Report to the Teaching & Learning Research Initiative Project. Wellington: Teaching Learning Research Institute/New Zealand Centre for Educational Research. Retrieved from http://www.tlri.org.nz/tlri-research/research-completed/ece-sector/whakawhanaungatanga%E2%80%94-partnerships-bicultural-development.

Skerrett, M. (2013). *The Politics of Pedagogical Darwinism*. Unpublished Conference Presentation: Christchurch, New Zealand: The Gathering, June 15, 2013.

Skerrett, M. (2010). A critique of the best evidence synthesis with relevance for Māori leadership in education. *Journal of Educational Leadership, Policy and Practice, 25*(1), 42–50.

Skerrett-White, M. N. (2003). *Kia mate rā anō a tama-nui-te-rā: Reversing Language Shift in kōhanga reo.* Unpublished doctoral thesis, Te Whare Wānanga o Waikato, University of Waikato, Hamilton.

Skerrett-White, M. N. (2001). The Rise and Decline of te Kohanga Reo: The Impact of Government Policy. In J. Ritchie, A. Parsonson, T. Karetu, N. Te Uira, & G. Lanning (Eds), *Te Taarere aa Tawhaki* (pp. 11–22). Hamilton: Waikato University College.

Te Rangi Hiroa (P. H. Buck). (1924). The passing of the Maori. *Transcations and Proceedings of the Royal Society of New Zealand 1868–1961, 55,* 362–375. Retrieved from http://rsnz.natlib.govt.nz/image/rsnz_355/rsnz_355_300_0440_0362_ac_0401.html.

Waitangi Tribunal. (1986). Report of the Waitangi Tribunal on the Te Reo Maori Claim (WAI 11). Wellington: GP Publications: Waitangi Tribunal. Retrieved from http://www.waitangi-tribunal.govt.nz/reports/default.asp?type=wai&keywords=11.

Waitangi Tribunal. (2010). Te Reo Māori. Wai 262. Pre publication report. Wellington: Waitangi Tribunal. Retrieved from http://www.waitangitribunal.govt.nz/scripts/reports/reports/262/056831F7-3388-45B5-B553-A37B8084D018.pdf.

Waitangi Tribunal. (2011). Ko Aotearoa Tēnei. A report into claims concerning New Zealand law and policy affecting Māori culture and identity. Te Taumata Tuarua. Volume 2. Wellington: Waitangi Tribunal. Retrieved from http://www.waitangi-tribunal.govt.nz/reports/downloadpdf.asp?ReportID={BF981901-5B55-441C-A93E-8E84B67B76E9}.

Waitangi Tribunal. (2012). Matua Rautia. Report on the Kōhanga Reo Claim. WAI 2336. Wellington: Waitangi Tribunal. Retrieved from http://www.waitangi-tribunal.govt.nz/reports/view.asp?reportId=8B60D3D9-A7F5-45B4-9605-F065D6645155.

Walker, R. (2004). *Ka Whawhai Tonu Matou: Struggle without End* (revised ed.). Auckland: Penguin.

Williams, D. (2004). Myths, national origins, common law and the Waitangi Tribunal. *Murdoch University Electronic Journal of Law, 11*(4). Retrieved from http://worldlii.austlii.edu.au/au/journals/MurUEJL/2004/2039.html.

Part A
Kaupapa Māori Early Childhood Care and Education

1
Dismantling Colonial Myths: Centralising Māori Language in Education

Mere Skerrett

Abstract: *This chapter explores some discourses shaping colonial thinking in Aotearoa. Implicit in Deleuze and Guattari's (2004) notions of deterritorialization is the restructuring of colonized space. Unmasking the power hierarchies (Cannella, 2011) of colonization serves to dismantle them. Alternative discourses speak to the conditions within which colonized peoples find themselves. It is argued that the re-generation of the Māori language in education is transformative. It repositions Māori knowledge/s at the core of curriculum. Transformative praxis (Freire, 1972) resists archaic teaching pedagogies, dismantles fixed truths, challenges knowledge monopolies, and troubles the hierarchical power structures that disadvantage indigenous children. Exposing the harmful effects of 'linguafaction' (a toxic byproduct of colonization) through discourse analysis strengthens the counter-colonial efforts of Māori language education in the early years.*

Ritchie J., and M. Skerrett. *Early Childhood Education in Aotearoa New Zealand: History, Pedagogy, and Liberation.* New York: Palgrave Macmillan, 2014.
DOI: 10.1057/9781137375797.0005

Introduction

New Zealand is a colonized country. Its institutions are British colonial imports. This chapter is concerned with countering colonization through a discourse analysis with a view to re-centering Māori language and knowledge in education. After Bevan-Smith (2012) through a discourse analysis we dehegemonize settler historiographies in New Zealand. We counter the effects of institutionalized racism, a feature of New Zealand schools that continue to position Māori children as being "in deficit." Even though the concept of "race" to me is based on an error of science—that is, assuming there are scientifically quantifiable qualities that amount to "race," the concept and associated discourses have powerfully shaped colonial institutions. Gannon argues the concept affords varying degrees of privilege and disadvantage to culturally diverse people (Gannon, 2009); Grosz argues that "the various distinctions and categories that mark race today are historically variable, politically motivated, and highly volatile in their operations" (quoted in Davies & Gannon, 2009, p. 71). As a British colony Māori in Aotearoa inherited the deficit colonial constructs of "Māori race" through its colonial discourses, its institutions, and its English language. Reality is both shaped by, and shapes, the languages we speak. Languages are dynamic forces. They create our realities in socio-cultural communities. Further, Gordon (2012) argues that we (people) are created in those realities that are social and cultural. He posits:

> Communication, at least at the level of human communication, requires social and cultural dimensions. These dimensions, as Frantz Fanon has argued in Black Skin, White Masks, are reservoirs of creativity, and the things they create are, in his words, sociogenic, that is, social in their origins. What this means is that the social world can create and eliminate kinds of people. Once created, the claim that their identities themselves [and languages] are the problems is a failure to address the social dynamics of their creation; it makes them the problems instead of the society that created them. (Gordon, 2012, p. 46)

The societal, systemic failure of Māori in the colonial and neocolonial education contexts of Aotearoa/New Zealand has led to, and reinforces, societal stratifications of disadvantage and privilege. In a foreign (for Māori at least) knowledge (English) system this is done through curricularly truncated practices designed within a pedagogy of erasure (of Māori knowledge and language). Ultimately these practices seek to colonize the Māori mind. In the sections below and chapters that follow in Part A, I will explain how Māori, as tāngata whenua (the people of the land), come to be positioned as "priority learners" with a strange twist that becomes apparent as we work through the discourses, policies, and practices in education.

Colonization and homogenization in education

Linda Smith's (1999) seminal book *Decolonizing Methodologies* backgrounds the contexts of indigenous peoples' lived experiences through the lens of colonization. She argues the "colony" is imperialism's outpost and makes important links between imperialism, history, writing, and theory. Firstly, she asserts, it is necessary to unpack "imperialism" for indigenous peoples. This is because it is imperialism that disrupts histories (indigenous peoples' stories) and radically alters indigenous peoples' lives. Imperialism is at the heart of empire-building, of the nation state. The notion that imperialism (and colonialism) is something only of the past is misconceived. Imperialism, according to Smith, is an ongoing project. "Imperialism still hurts, still destroys and is reforming itself constantly" (p. 19). Stewart-Harawira (2005) argues, "The reclaiming of invisibilized indigenous histories and the insurrection of subjugated indigenous cosmologies and ontologies are critical aspects of indigenous peoples' resistance to the homogenizing impulse of modernity and its manifestation in current forms of globalization" (p. 23). Indigenous (Māori) peoples have had to challenge colonial (in Aotearoa-powerful white British male) historians' views of the world. The establishment of new colonies through new settler populations and governments produces the establishment of new power—colonial power. Smith (1999) argued that the inherent (historical) racist underpinnings of colonial power in Aotearoa are alive and well. They arrived with the settlers and were hard-wired in settler institutions (churches, courts, prisons, governments, and schools. A recent Education Review Office (ERO)[1] publication (2012) discusses how ERO reviews have revealed curriculum neglect with teachers in control, who know little about their Māori students, their language/s, knowledge/s, nor what or how to teach them. It is argued here that many teachers hold on to colonial ideas of Māori "savagery," which is reflected in the way they think (and behave) toward Māori children. New Zealand education settings are full of teachers who adhere to the racist underpinnings of colonialism; they fail to acknowledge the relationships of language to learning, of pedagogies to people and place, of knowledge/s to curriculum, of mind to reality. Indeed many teachers just do not see or value the Māoriness in the Māori children in front of them. Instead they treat all children "the same" and tend not to respond to the aspirations and expectations of *whānau* Māori (ERO, 2010). In other words, they adhere to those core colonial beliefs as they actively subjugate the Māoriness in Māori children that are harmful. As Fanon (1967) puts it:

> Sometimes people hold a core belief that is very strong. When they are presented with evidence that works against that belief, the new evidence cannot be accepted. It would create a feeling that is extremely uncomfortable, called cognitive dissonance. And because it is so important to protect the core belief, they will rationalize, ignore and even deny anything that doesn't fit in with the core belief. (p. 194)

Indeed it is an ongoing struggle in education, across all sectors of education, when working towards changing educators' views, particularly when they are presented with evidence that works against their own educational experiences, language and knowledge systems, beliefs, values and practices, and when they may experience that *cognitive dissonance* which often presents itself as a barrier to change. But struggle is part of the change. Indigenous peoples have to understand that, and the mechanics of colonialism, how it impacts on all of our lives, and then create shared language/s for talking about it (Smith, 1999). Alternate discourses, from a strengths base, become a tool then to counter the effects of racism in education in an attempt to alleviate the harm that is caused to Māori children through the dissonance. That challenge is ongoing.

Power hierarchies through geographic territorialization and sociolinguistic stratification

"Ka tangi te tītī, ka tangi te kākā, ka tangi hoki ahau"
As the tītī (sooty shearwater) bursts forth, as the kākā (native parrot) assertively conducts;
a new day dawns and I too find my voice

Deleuze and Guattari's (1987) work (translated 2004), *A Thousand Plateaus: Capitalism and Schizophrenia*, the notion of *striated (stratified) space* assists with understanding the mechanics of colonization. The concept of striated space can be about the division of land; its objectification by surveying it, categorizing it, and putting up fences. This is the concept of territorialization. Likewise, striation can also be about the division of people who occupy those spaces. As spaces are territorialized, the people who occupy those territories are themselves territorialized (categorized) as they fit (or not) into those territories. Binaries are created. Davies (2009) argues, "The binaries become naturalized—the world is divided that way because it is that way—and they can create apparently insurmountable impediments to change" (Davies, 2009, p. 23). Binaries then create "normalities" and "abnormalities."

Territorialization is the commodification of land *and its inhabitants* and exemplified in McLintock's (1949) book, which gives a history of the colonization of Otago, New Zealand, drawing on many historical documents including Captain Cook's logs and other documents of the 1800s. He asserts:

> That Otago was destined to become the scene of a most interesting experiment in colonization did not even remotely enter his [Captain Cook's] mind. The land lay empty, unkempt and wild, and upon it rested still unbroken the silence of the centuries ... In the remote past the physical environment of a society was its dominant factor, and even among primitive people, such as the pre-European Māori, the human being was largely at the mercy of omnipotent nature. Natural phenomena dominated his thoughts, controlled his life and shaped his religion. In a very real sense, such history could be regarded as merely geography set in motion (p. 7).

The concept of natural phenomena dominating Māori thought, life, behavior, and spirituality is precise and is inextricably entangled in our expressive Māori language, which reflects just that—the interrelationality of the natural phenomena of Aotearoa/Otago and its Māori inhabitants. I would hypothesize that the languages of all indigenous peoples are connected in this way to the geography of the land. It makes sense that the first language mapped on to the land is that of the first people *on* that land—the idea that underpins the field of *terralinguistics* and is bound with the Māori terminology "tangata whenua" (people of the land). The following quote is intriguing:

> This does not mean that the historian is prepared to accept the absolute dictation of the geographical factor alone. He realizes, however, the need for an adequate study of any historical problem, first, as regards the action

of Nature on Man and, secondly, of equal or of greater importance, as regards the reaction of Man on Nature. Thus, if certain consequences follow certain causes, the explanation may well arise from human determination no less than from natural determinism. The colonization of Otago, which fell within the last century, gives excellent scope for such a two-fold investigation—the primitive environment, stark and unsympathetic, the pioneer society, eager to conquer and subdue. (p. 8)

The colonization of indigenous peoples is seen as the "historical problem." Of course by the time the British got around to colonizing Aotearoa/New Zealand, the European colonial tradition outside of Europe had been around for at least 500 years. In that sense the "problem" was somewhat historical; that being the extrication of the land out of people who are synchronized with the land. It was a violent process and one that had been fine tuned as indigenous peoples became a disposable by-product (of little consequence) in the productive territorialization of land to conquer it and to subdue it. Papatūānuku (our earth mother) became "it"; an apparatus for Western capitalist expansion. Furthermore, the following is a glimpse of what was awaiting the colonizers in 1948 when the first two ships for the Otago settlement arrived:

> It is difficult to-day ... to envisage the Otago landscape as it appeared to the pioneers, and—perhaps more difficult—to recapture the wonder it must have aroused within their minds. For those who assembled on the decks of the John Wickliffe and the Philip Laing to gaze with anxious eyes upon the land destined to be their home were greeted with a vista of what must have seemed an endless sweep of that sub-tropical rain forest, not the least among New Zealand's glories .... Even to land-hungry immigrants, the virgin beauty of the scene must have made a strong appeal until the soon familiar sound of axe and saw shattered the brooding spell of centuries. (p. 15)

We must remember here that my Ngāi Tahu (southern tribe) forebears had lived with this land for over a thousand years—had lived according to the principles of "kaitiakitanga" (give and take only what is needed) and manaakitanga (caring for the land)—but all too soon they struggled to protect their earth mother who sustained and provided their mahinga kai (food gathering places) once the settler colonizers arrived, exemplified in the corresponding disappearance of the forests and birds:

> But the unique experiences [of the settler pioneers] were all too fleeting and soon, very soon, a solitary bird-note became the echo of a once lovelier song. For it was a tragedy, little understood or heeded in those early decades,

that the native birds were fated to disappear at a rate corresponding to the destruction of the forest. (p. 22)

In discussion around the protection of mahinga kai with my 86-year-old father, he said, "Yes, yes, that's right—they had to protect all the mahinga kai—but what a shock with the arrival of the colonists. When our people stood at the Taiaroa Heads to welcome them in haka, they were shot at—many of them shot dead." Indigenous people were killed. Lands were carved up. The mellifluous dawn chorus vanished. The quote so aptly exemplifies the colonial/indigenous binaries Davies (2009) refers to, as if they are "natural" and "irrevocable":

- Māori as geography set in motion versus colonizers as motion set upon the geography
- Nature on Man versus Man on Nature
- Primitive environment (with primitive people) versus Subdued conquered environment (with civilized people)
- Natural determinism (people of the land) versus Human determination to conquer and control (people owning the land)
- Savage and unenlightened versus Urbane and civilized!

When the settler colonizers arrived, they did not find borders or survey pegs, or territories complete with cadastral maps establishing ownership for taxation/rates purposes. No, they saw rivers and trees and rocks and mountains and pristine lands, with multitudinous marae (ancestral homes and sacred lands) from Te Reinga (spiritual departing point at the northern tip of the North Island) to Kura Tawhiti (spiritual gathering place of Ngāi Tahu in the center of the South Island) to Te Kāreha-a-Tamatea (the southern tip of the South Island) and on all the surrounding islands. They met Māori people living with those lands and islands. The whole of Aotearoa/New Zealand was a marae to Māori, so when the Pākehā arrived at Taiaroa Heads and started to murder the welcoming haka-party the bitter memory lives on in the stories told by Ngāi Tahu elders today. Territorialization is a physical carving up of the land for categorization and stripping it of its people and resources. In the 1800s when the settlers arrived they did not find a territorialized country. They simply did not recognize the lands were governed by the relationships of the indigenous Māori people. Striation is part of the process of territorialization. It is the categorization element and for the purposes of this section it refers to the categorization (colonization) of language.

Language occupies physical space (Skerrett-White, 2003), in the mouths, on the tongues, and between the spaces of the people who speak those languages in the spaces they occupy. That the dawn chorus is impossible to re-enliven without its base (forest), so too it is nonviable to revitalize te reo Māori without a home base. Alongside Deleuzeguattarian theories of territorialization, striation of land peoples/land languages, I want to introduce the concept of *linguafaction*.

Linguafaction

As experienced recently in the series of extreme earthquakes in Christchurch, New Zealand, liquefaction happens during earthquakes when the ground shaking that occurs during the earthquake causes soils to liquefy. It is dangerous, ugly, and rank (to the nose), and occurs in seriously high-magnitude earthquakes. There are four main hazards from earthquakes: shaking, faulting, killer tidal waves, and ground failure (Alden, 2012). While all the hazards result from seismic movement, liquefaction is ground failure. It occurs in ground that has been seismically compromised and therefore is unsustainable for people to live on. It is full of contaminated water and ooze that, when it cements, is a health hazard. Linguafaction in this sense is akin to liquefaction. It occurs when Papatūānuku (our mother-land) co-modified through territorialization, through striation, is no longer able to sustain her indigenous populations, their ways of life, and their languages. This causes failures for indigenous peoples to thrive in their own homelands, their knowledge and value systems once solid now liquefied and their languages overcome by killer languages. Language shift through territorialization, like the land shift, creates the "linguafaction." It is precarious, traumatic, and discordant (to the ear). As in the earthquake zones where liquefaction makes the ground unsafe, in colonized zones linguafaction makes striated spaces unsafe. Smooth spaces where indigenous languages, cultures, and peoples thrived for millennia rapidly shift and disappear with colonization. The tāngata whenua (people of the land) suffer from introduced disease, culture shock, language loss, and temporal disorientation, and many die. Striated spaces are hazardous spaces for land, languages, and the people who use them. As Papatūānuku (mother-lands) are emasculated and territorialized, so too are the mother-tongues foremost mapped onto those lands (the terralingua). Language/s shift (from the terralingua of natural "smooth" environments to colonial language/s of unnatural territorialized space) is the fate of all indigenous languages living with linguafaction. Indigenous language/s undergo shift (from language of the land to foreign language) equivalent to the rate of shift of land from indigenous people/s to the colonizers. Territorialization disconnects indigenous languages from the landscape. It is the language/land disconnect that makes territorialized space unsafe for indigenous people and their languages that is termed here linguafaction. As I discussed earlier, as the native birds were fated to disappear at a rate corresponding to the destruction of the forest so too are indigenous languages fated to disappear at a rate corresponding to the territorialization of their lands.

Discourse analysis

French social theorist/philosopher Michel Foucault developed a notion of discourse in his early work, particularly in his influential 1972 text the *Archaeology of Knowledge*. Lessa (2006) proposes that Foucault's theorizing around the power of discourses emphasizes how they are implicated in the constitution of current *truths*, how they are *maintained* in societies, and what *power relations* they carry with them (p. 285). After Foucault, she refers to discourses as "systems of thoughts composed of ideas, attitudes, courses of actions, beliefs and practices that systematically construct the subjects and the worlds of which they speak" (p. 285). Furthermore, whilst some theorists propose different approaches to discourse analysis, they all start from the broadly accepted recognition that discursive power is what happens at the interactional level; that "language, the medium of interaction, creation and dissemination of discourses, is deeply implicated in the creation of regimes of truth, i.e. they explore ways in which, through discourses, realities are constructed, made factual and justified, bringing about effects" (Lessa, 2006, pp. 285–286).

Powerful discourses and society

Discourses are the medium of reality. They burst forth from theories and simultaneously are the foundries of theories. They are powerful and can be both diligent and dangerous in the way that they shape and misshape consciousness especially through mythological discourses presented as "truths," "fact," or "reality." Discourses are effective colonizing tools that can chisel through identities and hacksaw through traditional knowledge/s. This creates a "double-think" situation, resulting in cultural alienation. Tewa Pueblo Indian educator Gregory Cajete describes it as "cultural schizophrenia" (cited in Stewart-Harawira, 2005, p. 16). Ngugi Wa Thiong'o calls it "cultural annihilation" (1986). He asserts that the effect of this cultural bomb "is to annihilate a people's belief in their names, in their languages, in their environment, in their heritage of struggle, in their unity, in their capacities and ultimately in themselves" (Ngugi Wa Thiong'o, 1986, p. 3). Discourses (spoken and written) invent meanings between and among people, places, and things, and produce realities. Power relations are created among people and between diverse groups of people through their discourses. Discourses are produced by, and produce, the mechanics of society. They are powerfully productive and productively powerful. They are presented in schools as knowledge through the curriculum, and power through the teacher/student relationships.

Some of the current day discourses identified in this chapter (which are also located historically) employ discursive practices now deeply embedded into the fabric of our society, and that are re-productive. Through a discourse analysis involving a re-claiming and re-framing process, this chapter documents ways to create smooth spaces, in the Deleuze and Guattarian (2004) sense, in order to deterritorialize the language/landscape, to create lines of flight from the linguafaction that stultifies Māori language education. But it begs the paradoxical question: How does one influence (transform) ways of thinking that are deeply ingrained in the consciousness, which define reality, are productive, but which are not real and which are dissonant? Put simply, how does one smooth over striated spaces?

The individuality of a day (Tuck, 2010), a chance meeting in Wellington created a haecceity in a moment in relation to a report in *The Dominion Post*, a national paper located in our capital city, Wellington. Newspapers are present history tellers (Miller, 2008). *The Dominion Post* is no exception. It reflects the mythical colonial discourses that Ballara's (1986) text *Proud to be White? A Survey of Pākehā Prejudice in New Zealand* unpacks. Tracking current day discourses through Ballara's text allowed me to understand the process of how several colonial discourses have become internalized into the public consciousness (Skerrett, 2012; Skerrett, Ritchie, & Rau, 2013). I have selected three discourses that found their way that day into *The Dominion Post*. These discourses led me on a journey, in response to the present day "history-telling" of that national newspaper, and the *cognitive dissonance* they create. But they have their genesis in the myth-making discourses deeply embedded in the colonial agenda of invasion and territorialization. They are colonizing discourses, debunked here as colonizing falsehoods.

Myth one: we are all (happy) New Zealanders: trick or treaty

The Treaty of Waitangi[2] (2012) is one of the founding documents that laid the basis for British colonial settlement. There has been debate over its interpretation and meaning since it was first signed in 1840 to the present, with no unanimous Māori agreement (Orange, 2004). It takes its name from the place in the Bay of Islands where the debate first started between the British Crown and the Māori chiefs. As the Treaty of Waitangi established rights, so too did it test its first case in the newly established law courts. *R v Symonds* (Dorsett & Godden, 1998) established Māori rights to traditional land under customary law in 1847 (just seven years after signing the Treaty). The case held that Māori Treaty rights are founded, and must be guaranteed. That case created a challenge and much ire among the settlers who were hungry for land. Interestingly enough, that same year the *Education Ordinance*, 1847, introduced by Governor Grey, created the second challenge (the first being the ongoing debates around the language of the Treaty/Tiriti texts) for Māori in education when it decreed that English was compulsory in every school that was part of the system. It stated that schools: To be established or supported by public funds under the provisions of this Ordinance, religious education, industrial training, and instruction in the English language shall form a necessary part of the system to be pursued therein (New Zealand Legislative Council Ordinances, 1841–1853).

British settlers became angrier at the thought of Māori having land rights, thus restricting their movements. They put pressure on the government and land companies to secure more land for British settlement. Within a short time New Zealand was at war: a war between the British Crown and settlers and Māori, known as the Land Wars. These came to a peak in 1858, with the formation of the Kingitanga, the Māori King Movement, a resistance movement. In 1859, Henry Sewell, writing in his diary, crudely stated the mounting colonial view:The settlers, outnumbering the Maoris and stronger in a greater degree than the proportion of numbers, would not suffer their progress to be checked by an inferior race. They would, if necessary, take the land; the

Maoris would resist and be crushed or exterminated (cited in Ballara, 1986, p. 60).

Joseph Somes of the New Zealand Company, who maintained that it was the "right" of the British Crown to the "waste lands" of New Zealand, vulgarly wrote of intended deception around the Treaty:Made with naked savages by a consul invested with no plenipotentiary powers, without ratification by the Crown, [so that it] could [not] be treated by lawyers as anything but a praiseworthy device for amusing and gratifying savages for the moment (cited in Ballara, 1986, p. 36).

Not only were Māori "savage," Māori were seen as "*naked* savages," a convenient concept that would invalidate any treaty process as naked savages are incapable of entering into treaties. In New Zealand the people categorization and treaty rules were made up hurriedly in response to British settler desire. Further, as argued by Ballara (1986), Māori requests to address injustices were seen by patronizing colonialists as symptomatic of Māori inequality based in their implicit belief in white supremacy:

> To Europeans, a symptom of Māori inequality was what they liked to call the "privileges" enjoyed by the Māori people. In a debate in 1947 Sidney Holland ... pointed out that the Māori "enjoy many advantages; they enjoy special legislation; they enjoy special protection ... While these conditions obtain there cannot be equality of Māori with pakeha." (Ballara, 1986, p. 114)

Here is the twist. The discourse is an illogical bringing together of Māori as *naked savage*, perhaps *childlike*, certainly *inferior*, strangely blended with a Māori as *privileged* discourse as Māori attempts to retain land, to resist subjugation, and prevent further thefts were distorted as "proof" that Māori were "not equal." The thinking is "Māori are sub-humans who just want special privileges." These ideas were not new or even unique to Aotearoa/NewZealand. Fine-tuned in the colonization of the Americas, these discourses are also in line with the terra nullius discourses used in Australia by the British colonialists to claim sovereignty on the grounds that Australia was land belonging to no one; it was an unoccupied (vacant) space. With the nullius discourse the indigenous Australians were invisibilized, made to be sub-human. Therefore they were not entitled to live on their lands. Wherever they lived, it was through a privilege bestowed on them by the colonizer because of their savage/sub-human nature. This is a common feature of colonization where, as Bevan-Smith (2012) argues, the savage/civilized binary, congenital to European settlerism, underwrites its ideology of superior as well as acting as its mythopoeia (process of creating myths) for political purpose.

The unpopular (to British settlers) court ruling in 1847 in *Symonds's* case established Māori rights to traditional land under customary law, and combined with the deficit savage-type discourses created a context that led to the next well-known (among Māori communities) Treaty ruling of 1877 by Judge Prendergast. He found Aotearoa to be a territory inhabited only by *"savages"* and *"primitive barbarians"* and ruled that:Government must acquit itself ... of its obligation to respect native proprietary rights, and of necessity be the sole arbiter of its own justice ... [The Treaty] must be regarded as a simple *nullity*. No body politic existed capable of making cession of sovereignty ... [placing Māori] on the footing of foreigners ... Transactions with the natives for the cession of their title to the Crown are thus to be regarded as acts of State, and therefore are not examinable by any Court (Angelo, 2011, p. 156).

Between the *Symonds's* case and Judge Prendergast's ruling there has been a shift from Māori having rights in customary law to the nullification of Māori socio-political structures rendering Māori right-less. Here the nullius discourse takes form. Māori are positioned as "foreigners" and "aliens," allegedly incapable of treaty-making, just 37 years after the Treaty of Waitangi was signed. In a sharp twist, the guaranteed Treaty rights have shifted as the balance of power moved from Māori and their rangatiratanga rights to the settlers and their rights to settle. This rapidly accelerated colonization and rapidly impacted on Māori, now demographically thinned out and suffering from the variety of introduced diseases and illness. The "no rights/privilege" thinking is still around 150 years later, as in the following mythopoeic discourse:

> Quote from the Dominion Post, September 6, 2012
>
> **Letter: Taxpayers must withdraw funding**
> At least former prime minister Helen Clark and incumbent John Key have something in common: "no-one owns the water." Now we have Crown-funded entities dictating that one very privileged group [Māori] does own the water—and everything else they [the Māori] consider is theirs. Not much of what is claimed existed in 1840. The Maori Council, Waitangi Tribunal and chief funder for the huge Treaty claim industry, the Crown Forest Rental Trust, aren't elected at large.
>
> They are vested interest groups hell bent on destroying the country's unity with continued racist claims.

> Many millions have been paid in Treaty settlements since 1920 and for what?
> Nothing has changed for most Maori. Only the top 20 percent is doing well as they entrench themselves into positions of favour and privilege at everyone's expense.
> It's time we abolished the Maori seats, as well as the council, the tribunal and the CFRT.
> They should be like any other clubs, supporting themselves at their own expense.
> Then we might just have time to get back on to the Kiwi track and become one nation of peoples with the same rights and aspirations for everyone and a safe and secure future for all. (*The Dominion Post*, September 6, 2012)

The argument that "Māori don't have any rights" on the grounds that "not much existed in 1840" is not only illogical but fundamentally flawed. It is simply a fabrication to justify the "privilege" discourse and more, that Māori are "privileged racists." Then the fantasy kicks in—that "they (Māori) threaten the future security of our (white) country" when they (Māori) challenge Government neoliberal policies of privatization of state-owned assets. The fundamental flaw—a lie—then sets in train the mythical discourses and also sets the scene for ongoing societal tensions. These tensions are manufactured around the discourse that we are "all New Zealanders"; one homogenous group who speak one (English) language and Māori (with guaranteed Treaty rights) are somehow obliterated. There is also the subliminal promotion of the idea in the title (and expounded upon in the "them" and "us" of the text) that Māori don't pay taxes and are a drain on society at our (Pākehā) expense. The "them" and "us" of the discourse is necessary to keep the mechanics of racism operational. The following is the response of New Zealand Prime Minister John Key (Key, 2012) to Māori rights assertions in relation to the Treaty that demonstrate these ideas:

> And I think if you take the debate all the way back—my own personal view of this situation is that if you go back to 1840 when we signed the Treaty, the Crown as one partner agreed to preserve what would effectively establish property rights around land, forestry, and fisheries. What we also I think then said, well look, let's also make sure that all New Zealanders enjoy the same rights of being a New Zealander—the same capacity to access those rights but I think at that time we also—let's together, in partnership, build a

modern day New Zealand, and so if you accept that view point then I think you have to accept that elements like water, and wind and sun and air and fire and all these things, sea, along with natural resources like oil and gas, are there for the national interest of everyone. They are for the benefit of all new Zealanders, not one particular group over another. (TVNZ, September 2012)

The text is "the Treaty was made between the Crown for and on behalf of *all New Zealanders*." The subtext is "therefore all New Zealanders own everything and you (Māori) have no rights as long as you continue to be that—'Māori.'" Somehow, according to Key, you cannot be a New Zealander and a Māori because being a New Zealander means giving up your Māoritanga (Māori cultural identity) and ceding all rights. Therefore the Treaty doesn't even concern you (Māori) because it is about *all New Zealanders* generally, not Māori specifically. Therein lies the Treaty twist—with one *magic* wave of the wand Māori have been totally invisibilized—such is the trickery of the treat-y.

Myth two: colonization is benevolent; therefore Māori ungrateful

In the Foreword to Ballara's (1986) book, Hiwi Tauroa, former New Zealand Race Relations Conciliator, wrote that behind the expression "You Maoris are lucky that we English took over" is an unconsciously sown and carefully but continually nurtured attitude of the English culture that there is only one culture which expresses all that is good for "other," and "all people" (p. ix). Ballara points out that in the 1960s and 1970s the contention was popular; where there are two main cultures, one must give way. Because Māori culture is cultivated as "primitive," "intellectually stagnant," and altogether unsuited to the twentieth century, it (Māori) must give way. Moreover, while giving way, Māori had better acknowledge the benefits that have been bestowed on them by the "benevolent (British) benefactor," the sentiments of which can be seen in the following *Listener* article 40 years ago:

> The Māori has not yet left the seventeenth century. No wonder he is in trouble. He is trying to match seventeenth century concepts with twentieth century technology ... We will not change to suit the Māori. He has to change if he wants to enter the twentieth century. (cited in Ballara, 1986, p. 164)

The underlying premise is that "Māori are practically Stone Age people and ought to be grateful for colonization which brought them out of the

Stone Age and, if ungrateful, we can put them straight back there." The following discourse perpetuates that myth that Pākehā colonization is good for Māori who ought to be grateful because they are Stone Age and would have remained solidified but for colonial invasion:

> Quote from the Dominion Post, September 6, 2012
>
> **Letter: How Irish and Māori histories diverge.**
> However, there are also significant differences between the two histories [Irish and Māori]. Ireland/Eire and its people were, in many ways, at least as "advanced" as the British and received virtually nothing of value from their oppressors.
> Maori, on the other hand [not advanced], have benefited enormously from a wide range of inventions and enterprise introduced from the northern hemisphere.
> So, though Maori justifiably seek redress for what was taken from them, it would be pleasing to occasionally hear some expressions of gratitude for the many benefits they've received from Pakeha.
> Or would they prefer that everything be just as it was before the foreigners arrived? (*The Dominion Post*, September 6, 2012)

This is yet another iteration of the "privilege" discourse, and illustrates the reach of the particular type of colonization—that of the British. What is even more insidious is the underlying assumption that Māori, "not advanced," can only "advance" as determined by the other, that is, locked into a past/present, without futures. It is plainly a dehumanizing discourse full of Eurocentric ideology, with an underpinning denial of the right of the "other" people to self-determine.

And the British shall inherit the earth

The popular discourse promulgated in the earliest days of the colony's formation is that the British were the *"natural God given heirs"* of New Zealand, and it should belong to them on the grounds of their being superior and "economically productive" whereas Māori were "non-productive" natives, as exemplified in the following:

> The Natives subsist on the food we have brought them, pork and potatoes; and till we came, they wandered over a fair portion of the earth, without knowing the use of it. Before that the only animals they had to eat, except themselves, were rats, and their only fruit, poor wild berries. (Ballara, 1986, p. 47)

Ballara (1986) argued that this was of course promoted to deny Māori rights and was in direct contrast to the realities of the time when in fact many settlers in Auckland and Wellington were dependent on the food supplies cultivated and brought to market by the Māori. However, this recurring theme, both historically and currently, is that it was the British who bestowed the economic value to land and its resources, therefore Māori have no rights to economic advancement (because Māori can just revert to eating rats and berries). This idea was typical in the early colonial period because Māori were very successful traders, farmers, and millers, and were budding capitalists in the fishing and shipping industries. Māori productivity was therefore seen as a threat to British colonization. The theme of Māori having no rights to control land interests (and therefore economic productivity) is highlighted in the following types of discourse that surfaced in the early 1900s regarding Māori rental properties: "It seemed that to seek the most advantageous commercial terms was somehow disgraceful in a Māori, and could only be tolerated in civilised capitalists" (p. 80). This same theme is highlighted in the following discourse:

Quote from the Dominion Post, September 6, 2012

Letter: Government must reject Māori claims
OPINION: The Waitangi Tribunal has found that Maori have rights to water. Why? Because it has been "commercialised" by passing through a power turbine. And why is commercialised water any different from other water? Maori didn't process water in 1840, so can't have had a customary claim to commercialised water ... Water that has been treated for human consumption is also commercialised. If Maori own water that is commercialised through a turbine, they also have a claim to drinking water. There is actually a stronger argument with drinking water, because it retains its commercial character, and doesn't become waste water straight away, as hydro-water does.

If Maori have an interest in water commercialised by others, it doesn't follow that they also have an interest in the power companies using that water. Or does the companies' brief use of "Maori water" make that power company part Maori-owned? The tribunal apparently thinks so.

By its logic, Maori would also have an interest in water utilities and our own houses, because we all use tap water. The idea that anyone owns water, and that rights to water lead to rights to other property, is illogical and must be rejected. (*The Dominion Post*, September 6, 2012)

This discourse is a good illustration of how the public consciousness can be beguiled into a false consciousness. The central issue—the selling out of our country—has been totally misrepresented as a public good and when Māori challenge the government monopoly of Māori lands and resources, and the government neoliberal agenda to sell out for profit (for the benefit of a few) and privatization, Māori are somehow made to look like the villains. Another irony: the government is still enforcing, though not explicitly, what it perceives to be its Treaty right of pre-emption[3] on the one hand while it scandalously dishonors the Treaty on the other, through ongoing lands and resource confiscations.

Māori, constantly vilified in the media (a trend set down historically), are invariably positioned in the binary of enemy of the state (Māori), friend of the people (Pākehā view/policy), so that when an issue raised by Māori is played out in the public sphere there is an automatic default mechanism positioning that issue as "bad" and therefore "Māori" as "bad." This is how the public consciousness is shaped. Māori claims are continuously presented in the media as contravening the general public interest' as if Māori, "the enemy," are somehow not part of the public interest. But the actuality is that Māori serve as exceptional critics and conscience of society. Many Māori, tirelessly skeptical, tend to question the perceived views apparent in media discourse; the motives of press and indeed powerful politicians; as to whether or not they purport to represent the interests of Māori and the public good. That is the critical element of Māori people's resistance to the homogenizing impulse of modernity that Stewart-Harawira (2005) spoke of. Since the signing of the Treaty of Waitangi, critical analysis has been hardwired into the DNA of Maoridom.

Myth three: what? racism in New Zealand, never!

Historically, it has been argued by Ballara (1986), there has always been a color bar in New Zealand albeit a de facto one, evident in the ways in which some theatres, bars, and restaurants discriminated against Māori; how Māori were not welcome in Pākehā social institutions; Māori women being discouraged from entering the public restrooms; community centers being regarded as a facilities for Europeans only; differing rates of pay and job opportunities; and discrimination in the work place, housing, and so on. However, in spite of the frequency with which the reality of a color bar in New Zealand was demonstrated, there has persisted a myth, promoted publicly and maintained officially, that New Zealand was/is a "prejudice-free" country, in which Pākehā and Māori lived together in peace and harmony; that, after all New Zealand is a fair-minded, free, and independent Nation. In the following discourse clearly the analysis lacks some awareness but, by virtue of its publication, keeps the mythologizing mechanisms productive:

> Quote from the Dominion Post, September 6, 2012
>
> **Letter: He has no right to use that word**
> OPINION: African-Americans earned the right to call each other "nigger." They earned it through suffering real oppression at the hands of die-hard racists.
> Mana Party leader Hone Harawira (Harawira's N-bomb directed at National MPs, Stuff, September 6) has no such right. He isn't black, he isn't African-American, he hasn't suffered anything like the same oppression. On the contrary, he's benefited from one of the most relatively benevolent colonizations of the 18th and 19th century.
> All he is [is] a racist Maori serial complainer. He wallows in his perception of past wrongs because he doesn't have anything else to offer. He'll remain a gathering point for his, mercifully, few fellow travellers and a figure of repulsion for the rest of us. (*The Dominion Post*, September 6, 2012)

As Tuck (2010) argues, there are inconsistencies and tensions in defining indigeneity as blood-quantum bound or any other external definition, for example, skin color. Gordon (2012) asserts that the formulation of black and white worlds does not refer to every individual black or white person, but to those who live by the value systems of those worlds. Further, that "whereas whiteness relies on a narcissistic self-deceptive notion of the American social and political system's completeness, blackness relies on pointing out the incompleteness of the system, its imperfections and contradictions" (Gordon, 2012, p. 8). Here is one contradiction made explicit in the above discourse: *benevolent colonizations* the oxymoron of a "kind violent" process, the logic of which underpins ethnocentrism and provides some insight into the "kiwi" consciousness. Māori must continue, at every bend, to resist discourses that promote "whiteness" and territorialize Māori identities through external discourses of blood-quantum, skin color or skull size, bone density, hair characteristic, name-calling, and labeling or any other such objectifying apparatus. They are the apparatuses of anti-Māori racism. An effective tool, a resource, that counters anti-Māori racism is the promotion and revitalization of the Māori language because it is through the reo Māori that alternative discourses surface.

Conclusions

This chapter foregrounds some of the inherent racist underpinnings of colonization entrenched in the New Zealand consciousness through its daily discourses. This consciousness is what underpins our societal institutions and, crucially, educational practices. It is a difficult thing to acknowledge that our education system is inherently racist, facilitated through teachers in denial, but who readily admit that they know little about their Māori students (ERO, 2012). As Gordon (1995) puts it:

> A great deal of the effort to study racism is marred by the core problem of self-evasion. This is partly because the study of racism is dirty business. It unveils things about ourselves that we may prefer not to know. If racism emerges out of an evasive spirit, it is hardly the case that it would stand still and permit itself to be unmasked. (p. ix)

The self-evasion in New Zealand's history has been referred to as sociohistorical *amnesia* (Walker, 1990) and is the means by which colonial status quo of unequal power relations is maintained. The serious issue of the negative impacts of anti-Māori racism in education is deeply imbued at the ideological level in "Whitestream" New Zealand. It is argued that implicit in colonizer worldviews there is an assumed power to define their worldviews as "truth," "facts," "scientific," corresponding to a generalized reality fit for curriculum packaging in education. Concomitantly, Māori worldviews are seen as "savage," "unenlightened," "myths," even "lies," fit only for eradication or museums. This explains why, and the ways in which, Māori knowledge was misappropriated and misrepresented in education (Smith, 1999). The education system in New Zealand is a key mechanism for the maintenance of anti-Māori racism. It is systemically and systematically corrupt.

Deleuzeguattarian theories assist in critically analyzing Māori experience with what has been termed territorializing, deterritorializing, and reterritorializing. Implicit in Deleuze and Guattari's (1987) notions of reterritorialization is the restructuring of a territorialized space in order to dismantle the patriarchal hierarchies of colonization creating smoother spaces to navigate. The smooth spaces allow for Māori to stand on their tūrangawaewae, to elevate themselves on the shoulders of their ancestors to see their future pathways, to distinguish the navigational landmarks and fertile grounds to continue to build marae. Smooth spaces allow for liberatory praxis. They stimulate the imagination and facilitate transformation. Juxtaposing these Deleuzeguattarian notions therefore assist with theorizing the colonization of Aotearoa (through land commodification), and the cultural shock impacting on Māori as "tāngata whenua" and Māori language through linguafaction.

It has been argued that language/s shift (from the terralingua of natural "smooth" environments to colonial territorialized space) is the fate of all indigenous languages living with linguafaction. Indigenous language/s undergo shift equivalent to the rate of shift of land from indigenous people/s to the colonizers for their institutional developments. Territorialization disconnects indigenous languages from the landscape, their lives, and their languages. It is the language/land disconnects that makes territorialized space unsafe for indigenous people and their languages that is argued occurs through linguafaction.

Further, colonial discursive practices create a false consciousness through myth-making discourses. Attempts to eliminate Māori identities (and language) through colonization have created severe socio-cultural dislocation for many Māori. Counter-colonial (Māori) spaces and readings of texts allow for alternative ways of thinking, knowing, and being in the world and seek to counter such dislocation.

Just one day in the life of *The Dominion Post*—September 6, 2012—displayed an entire two-page foldout of eurocentrism extraordinaire, full of harmful discourses "masking the power hierarchies" (Cannella, 2011) of colonization. Not only were Māori seemingly "savage," Māori were seen as "*naked* savages." The categorization of Māori thus, not as "sovereign people" was merely a maneuver to *lock* Māori into a state of being "incapable of maturation—needs tutelage" (Gordon, 2012). The Stone Age myth promotes the idea that Māori were "frozen in time" and therefore "without futures" is fundamentally an *error* of logic. The dehumanizing discourses consigning Māori people to "savage sub-humanhood" were merely attempts to invade and invalidate the Treaty, largely in response to British settler discontent over their insatiable demands for land. That these types of discourses are still in vogue today show that the discontent continues and is inculcated into the "kiwi" psyche. The Treaty spin that it was made between the Crown for and on behalf of *all New Zealanders* simultaneously invisibilizing Māori is the ultimate "treaty trick."

How some discourses create realities has been tracked drawing on three historical myth-making discursive practices to current day ones. This analysis followed those discourses with a view to showing how they become entrenched through continuous streams of consciousness played out in current day history-making media mechanisms, for the purposes of this chapter, newspapers, and educational settings. In this way they become self-perpetuating discourses. Discourse analysis is an effective tool that provides push-back to the insidiousness of internalized colonial thought. *Reterritorialization* as a theoretical frame can assist with the re-framing of a new "whare" or "marae" (spiritual homelands) through the creation of te ao Māori spaces.

The parallel discourses in which the colonization of Aotearoa New Zealand is viewed as a wholly positive thing that brought civilization and benefits to Māori provided opposing discourses based on the view that colonization was harmful, destructive, and destabilizing for Māori: a wholly negative thing. This has been a discourse analysis of power, hierarchy, exploitation, harm, and survival. Even though New Zealand is no longer a Dominion of England, the imperialist footprints remain. Unpacking how discursive myths become internalized has been a straightforward task. How we disrupt them is perhaps not so easy, but we *do not* have to tacitly, uncritically, accept the current status quo as *inevitable*, as natural, as "normal." We *do not* have to accept the monocultural, monolingual, foreign view the world. The words used in colonial discourses express the myth-making and the culturally different worldviews bound up with the language of the colonizers. Counter-colonial discourses represent the unmasking of anti-Māori racism, a struggle for power, and the reterritorialization of Aotearoa. The following two chapters will look at Māori language regeneration and its official introduction into all facets of municipal life, especially education.

Notes

1 The ERO is an independent government department that reviews the performance of schools and early childhood services, and reports publicly on what it finds.
2 Further expanded on in Chapter 2.
3 An Article II Treaty right of pre-emption in the Crown which, to the British, meant Māori gave up the right directly negotiate land deals with settlers, the Crown thus creating a monopoly on the purchase of Māori land.

References

Alden, A. (2012). http://geology.about.com/od/liquefaction/a/liquefaction.htm (accessed December 4, 2012).

Angelo, A. H. (2011). *Constitutional law in New Zealand*. The Netherlands: Kluwer Law International.

Bevan-Smith, J. (2012). *The new cannibal club: Deconstructing history in Aotearoa New Zealand*. Unpublished doctoral thesis. University of Auckland, New Zealand.

Ballara, A. (1986). *Proud to be White? A Survey of pākehā prejudice in New Zealand*. Auckland, NZ: Heinemann Publishers.

Cannella, G. (2011). Political possibility, hypercapitalism, and the "Conservative Reeducation Machine." *Cultural Studies: Critical Methodologies, 11*, 364. Published online. Doi: 10.1177/1532708611414667.

Davies, B. (2009). Difference and differentiation. In B. Davies & S. Gannon (Eds), *Pedagogical Encounters*. New York: Peter Lang.

Davies, B., & Gannon, S. (Eds) (2009). *Pedagogical Encounters*. New York: Peter Lang.

Deleuze, G., & Guattari, F. (2004). *A Thousand Plateaus: Capitalism and Schizophrenia* (B. Massumi, Trans.). London & New York: Continuum (Original work published 1987).

Dorsett, H., & Godden, L. (1998). *A Guide to Overseas Precedents of Relevance to Native Title*. Canberra: Aboriginal Studies Press for the Australian Institute of Aboriginal and Torres Strait Islanders Studies.

Education Review Office. (2010). *Success for Māori Children in Early Childhood Services*. Available http://learn.canterbury.ac.nz/file.php/3101/Bilingual_Ed_Readings2012/success-maori-ece-may10_1_.pdf

Education Review Office. (2012). *Evaluation at a Glance: Priority Learners in New Zealand Schools*. Available http://www.ero.govt.nz/National-Reports/Evaluation-at-a-Glance-Priority-Learners-in-New-Zealand-Schools-August-2012.

Fanon, F. (1967). *Black Skin, White Masks*. London and Sydney: Pluto Press.

Foucault, M. (1972). *The Archaeology of Knowledge*. Great Britain: Tavistock Publications.

Freire, P. (1972). *Pedagogy of the Oppressed*. Penguin.

Gannon, S. (2009). Difference and ethical encounter. In B. Davies & S. Gannon (Eds), *Pedagogical Encounters*. New York: Peter Lang.

Gordon, L. R. (1995). *Bad Faith and Antiblack Racism*. NJ: Humanities Press International, Inc.

Gordon, L. (2012). African-American Philosophy, Race, and the Geography of Reason. http://www.youtube.com/watch?feature=player_embedded&v=Vqn3tr9V-1Y#t=24s (accessed December 4, 2012).

Key, J. (2012, September). Prime Minister's response to Māori rights assertions in relation to the Treaty. *TVNZ*.

Lessa, I. (2006). Discursive struggles within social welfare: restaging teen motherhood. *British Journal of Social Work, 36*, 283–298.

Letter: He has no right to use that word. *(September 6, 2012)*. The Dominion Post, Letter.

Letter: How Irish and Māori histories diverge. *(September 6, 2012)*. The Dominion Post, Letter.

Letter: Taxpayers must withdraw funding. *(September 6, 2012)*. The Dominion Post, Letter.

McLintock, A. G. (1949). *The History of Otago. Otago* Centennial *Historical* Publications, NZ: Dunedin.

Miller, R. J. (2008). *Native America, Discovered and Conquered: Thomas Jefferson, Lewis and Clark, and Manifest Destiny*. Lincoln and London: University of Nebraska Press.

New Zealand Legislative Council Ordinances 1841–1853, Public Ordinance No. X (pp. 73–74). Wellington, NZ: Government Printer.

Ngugi Wa Thiong'o. (1986). *Decolonizing the Mind: The Politics of Language in African Literature*. London: James Currey.

Orange, C. (2004). *An Illustrated History of the Treaty of Waitangi*. Wellington, NZ: Bridget Williams Books.

Skerrett, M. E. (2012). *Countering Colonization—Māori Language Revitalization in Aotearoa*. Unpublished conference presentation, Pennsylvania State University, USA.

Skerrett, M. E., Ritchie, J., & Rau, C. (2013). *Kei tua i te awe māpara: Counter-colonial unveiling of neoliberal discourses in Aotearoa New Zealand*. Special Issue 7(2).

Skerrett-White, M. E. (2003). *Kia Mate Rā Anō A Tama-nui-te-rā: Reversing Language Shift in Kōhanga Reo*. Unpublished doctoral thesis, University of Waikato, New Zealand.

Smith, L. (1999). *Decolonizing Methodologies: Research and Indigenous Peoples.* NY: Zed Books Ltd.

Stewart-Harawira, M. (2005). *The New Imperial Order.* Wellington, NZ: Huia Publishers.

Treaty of Waitangi. (2012). *The Treaty of Waitangi.* Retrieved from http://www.nzhistory.net.nz/files/documents/treaty-kawharau-footnotes.pdf

Tuck, E. (2009). Re-visioning action: participatory action research and indigenous theories of change. *Urban Review, 41,* 47–65.

Tuck, E. (2010). Breaking up with Deleuze: desire and valuing the irreconcilable. *International Journal of Qualitative Studies in Education, 23*(5), 635–650.

Walker, R. (1990). *Ka whawhai tonu matou: Struggle Without End.* Auckland, NZ: Penguin Books.

2
Policy and Inhibiters of Bicultural/Bilingual Advancement

Mere Skerrett

Abstract: *This chapter frames the context in which Kaupapa Māori education, particularly that of Te Kōhanga Reo (bilingual/immersion early years language nests), has emerged. It commences with an exploration of some of the socio-historical legal and political developments defining the context of Māori education broadly, and bilingual/immersion early childhood care and education (ECCE) specifically. It provides an analysis of policy documents, principally the first early childhood strategy* Pathways to the Future *(Ministry of Education, 2002). It asserts that this strategy was designed to shape the direction of both Kaupapa Māori ECCE and the* whitestream *sector, but that it was more about coercing the Māori medium sector back into the mainframe of* whitestream *provision. It also emphasizes the long-lasting effects of colonialism on Māori societies and culture, the intergenerational disruption of knowledge transmission, and the devastating effects on Māori language loss. Māori language education is in crisis.*

Ritchie J., and M. Skerrett. *Early Childhood Education in Aotearoa New Zealand: History, Pedagogy, and Liberation.* New York: Palgrave Macmillan, 2014.
DOI: 10.1057/9781137375797.0006.

> E ngā rangatira, whakarongo mai!
> Kaua e ūwhia Te Tiriti o Waitangi i te kahu o Ingarangi,
> ēngari kia mau anō ki tōu kahu,
> te kahukiwi o Aotearoa nei.
>
> > Nā Aperahama Taonui, 6 o ngā rā o Hui Tānguru, 1840
> > (Cited in Ngā Haeata Mātauranga, 1994)
>
> *(To all dignified gatherers, take heed! Do not veil Te Tiriti o Waitangi with the shroud of England, but hold on to your unique cloak, the kiwi-feathered cloak of Aotearoa)*

Introduction

Bilingual immersion centers in early years' education within Aotearoa/New Zealand are transformative (Skerrett-White, 2003). There is now a full stream of Māori immersion education spanning what we call the non-compulsory sector (early childhood education—ECE) and compulsory sectors (primary/elementary through to secondary). Defining the terms "bilingualism" and "bilingual education" is difficult. May (2010) clarifies the term *bilingual education* because he asserts that it has widely different understandings. He places bilingual education on a continuum. At one end of the continuum there are those who would classify teaching bilingual students as bilingual education, irrespective of their educational aims (fostering bilingualism or not). At the other end of the continuum are those who distinguish between assimilatory (subtractive) programs and strong bilingual (additive) programs. Teachers need to understand the distinctions between weak and strong bilingual education in order to differentiate provision. Māori immersion settings are bilingual settings, *not* because they use two languages in the program, but because they are supporting bilingualism as an outcome (Skerrett-White, 2003) in Māori-medium programs. This is often misunderstood in New Zealand. Immersion programs are bilingual programs with bilingual aims and outcomes; the optimum percentage for quality early years' immersion education in the Aotearoa New Zealand context is between 90 and 100 percent in the target language (May, 2010).

That said, public policy has been slow to keep up with the rapid pace of change, resulting in a paucity of support, policy, and curriculum development, for bilingual/immersion settings, the largest provider of which is

Kōhanga Reo (Māori immersion language nests). This is what has come to be known as a "flax-roots" movement, and is now partially state-funded under the Crown[1]-regulated mainstream ECE sector (Waitangi Tribunal, 2012). This chapter explores some legal and political developments together with several relevant policy documents impacting on the context of Māori education broadly and Māori immersion ECE specifically. It is argued here that the hegemonic policies of the past have had negative influences on the bilingual/immersion education sector, such that the whilst the new *Māori Language in Education Strategy 2013–2017* (Ministry of Education, 2013b) is meant to provide a glimmer of hope, the policy does not go far enough in my view, and therefore is unlikely to have any meaningful impact or influence for Māori bilingual/immersion provision in early years' education. This chapter commences with an overview of the colonial context of Declaration and Treaty signing and the ensuing discourses over the intervening years.

The 1835 Declaration of Independence and 1840 Te Tiriti o Waitangi

A central thread woven through this book is a critique of Aotearoa becoming a colony of England. England is a common law[2] country where customary rights were founded. New Zealand was annexed (to New South Wales) in 1839 and the laws of England applied as at January 1840 (Webb, Sanders, & Scott, 2010). In international law a settled country must recognize the customary rights of the native people. In 1835 *He Wakaputanga o te Rangatiratanga o Nu Tirene: A Declaration of the Independence of New Zealand* was signed between the Rangatira (chiefly nobles) and the King of England; sovereignty over Aotearoa/ New Zealand lay with the Chiefs of the United Tribes (Mutu, 2010). That Declaration (drafted by the same person who drafted The Treaty of Waitangi five years later) used the words *kingitanga* and *mana* to mean *sovereignty* and *kawanatanga* for *government*. The 1840 Treaty of Waitangi did not.

There were several Treaty versions (referred to as English and Māori texts). They are not translations of each other but distinct documents with, in many respects, oppositional meanings. The Māori text was what the Rangatira (sovereign chiefs) understood and the one almost all of them signed. It is important to understand this pre-treaty context,

DOI: 10.1057/9781137375797.0006

particularly the words used in the *Declaration of Independence* to mean sovereignty (*kingitanga* and *mana*) and government (*kawanatanga*) because it provides some clarity around Māori understandings at the time of the signing of the Treaty. The 1835 Declaration of Independence and the 1840 Treaty of Waitangi documents were virtually back to back in time as signatures were still being collected for the Declaration in 1839 when the Treaty of Waitangi was being drafted. By 1839, 52 *sovereign powered* chiefs (acknowledged by the King and British government) had signed the *Declaration of Independence*, which was seen by James Busby as a significant mark of Māori national identity, and which would prevent other countries from making formal deals with Māori (The 1835 Declaration of Independence, 2013). It was gazetted internationally by Great Britain, which meant that in international law the world recognized mana Māori (Māori sovereignty) so that the English were at liberty to broker the relationship. While I refer to "the Treaty" in a general sense, it is to the rights and interests validated and guaranteed in "Te Tiriti o Waitangi" (the Māori text) that this chapter refers to.

The preamble to the Māori text establishes preservation of Tino Rangatiratanga (absolute authority) and the nature of the agreement (The Queen's governance). However, the English text recognizes Her Majesty's sovereign authority. Kawharu (2013) discusses the differences in the texts and the following articles: Article the First of the Māori text establishes that *governance* (not ceding sovereignty) was given over to the Queen of England in the Māori text. However, in the English text, whilst simultaneously acknowledging the sovereign rights and powers of the Individual Chiefs "*over their respective Territories as the sole sovereigns thereof*," it states that they ceded that sovereignty to the Queen of England. Both English and Māori texts in Article the Second protect the Chiefs and Hapū in the exercise of their Rangatiratanga (sovereignty) over lands, villages, and treasures so long as Māori wish to retain them, establishing pre-emption rights for the Crown. Article the Third guaranteed the protection of Māori dual rights as tāngata whenua and the same rights and duties of citizenship as the people of England.

There was no question that the preamble to the Māori text established that a government was being set up and that the sovereign power of chiefs was guaranteed. Arguably the biggest debate around the English and Māori texts is the question of what was ceded in Article II—*sovereignty* in the English text or *governance* in the Māori text; but in any event, in international law the Māori text is *the* legal document and trumps the foreign (English) text (see the Law of Contra Proferentem), settling the moot point—*governance* was ceded.

In 1840 the Māori chiefs held the mana whenua (land sovereignty); they exercised control over their lands, which spanned the whole country. Aotearoa/New Zealand was Māori land and Māori chieftainship was sovereign. Why would a previously declared independent nation of powerful sovereign chiefs then collaborate in their own subjugation through a treaty of cession as some commentators assert the Treaty of Waitangi purports to be? That simply did not happen. What did happen subsequently was a series of deliberate, fraudulent misrepresentations in duplicitous interactions through the settler system of government established post Treaty. Colenso reported that the English present at Waitangi in 1840 became agitated about the missionaries not translating or explaining the English version of the Treaty that they had drafted (Mutu, 2010). Māori were dubious of the tikanga (rules, values, and procedures of engagement) practiced by the British. As it turned out, deception and misrepresentation were part of that tikanga process by the outsider adventitious British. By placing the Māori language document in front of the Māori chieftainship to sign, whilst deceitfully drawing up a different (English language) version (not put to the Chieftainship) is a show of such deception. There were several legal and political developments in terms of Treaty jurisprudence from the signing of the Treaty of Waitangi in 1840 to the present day that have impacted heavily on Māori political, educational, and social advancements.

It has been shown (see Chapter 1) how in the case of *R v Symonds*,[3] Māori rights to traditional land under customary law were established in 1847 (Mutu, 2010). This case is famous for the common law doctrine of aboriginal (customary) title, meaning the right of Māori to claim a legal interest in their traditional lands must be respected (Webb, Sanders, & Scott, 2010). Chapman J. stated that *"if [native title] is entitled to be respected ... [it] cannot be extinguished ... otherwise than by the free consent of the Native occupiers"* (p. 214), and that Māori sovereignty and dominion over land was to be respected. What happened in the ensuing years? The settler population grew exponentially, land wars broke out between Māori and the setter government, and the Kingitanga (Māori King Movement) was established, resulting in British backlash. The reprisal for the establishment of a Māori King Movement was Māori land confiscations on a massive scale. Accompanying the rate of land confiscations (freed up for successive waves of British settlers to take over) was a shift in Māori language use as a result of *linguafaction* (see Chapter 1). Māori became increasingly disempowered. Māori language was weakened. Fishman (1991) has argued that, without a doubt, "weakened and endangered languages pertain to cultures that no longer significantly regulate the daily lives of their members" (p. 8). Along with land and language loss we have cultural loss, a loss in unique values and worldview/s and intergenerational trauma as generations of Māori were socio-culturally dislocated via ongoing colonization and through assimilative educational policy. The following is an exposé and critical analysis of the policy documents that continue to inhibit Māori language education generally and particularly in the early years.

The Treaty of Waitangi and the 1987 Lands Case

> *Waiho mā te ture, te ture e aki*
> *nā Te Kooti Rikirangi*
> Abandon futile acts; it is through the instrument of the law
> that the law will be instrumentalized

Within just seven years of signing the Treaty of Waitangi a case for customary title was established in the Courts, yet 30 years later there was a complete turnaround. In 1877 the Court established the Treaty as a nullity. Ngāti Toa leader *Wi Parata* had taken a case against the Bishop of Wellington for misuse of lands gifted for a specific purpose, the establishment of an educational setting for Ngāti Toa (see *Wi Parata v Bishop of Wellington* (1877) 3 NZ Jur (NS) SC 78). The judge Prendergast C. J. found there was no land gift from Ngāti Toa to the Bishop of Wellington because the Crown was found to own all the land by virtue of discovery and occupation. Here is blatant fraudulence. He also found these lands to be a territory inhabited only by *savages*, and that New Zealand was acquired through discovery and occupation—clearly a fabrication. That proprietary rights belonged to Māori were ignored. The ruling by the Court in the 1877 *Wi Parata* case effectively prevented Māori from successfully protecting their proprietary rights through the New Zealand Courts. For 110 years, from 1877 to 1987, the different versions of the Treaty created different pathways, leading to different outcomes for Māori and Pākehā; the Crown and its settler government (and successions of English settlers) recognizing the duplicitous English version (denying the declaratory law of Te Tiriti o Waitangi; maintaining a treaty of cession), and benefitting from the legal and political developments (wars, dominion over land and resources, and institutionalized power). Māori recognizing the *legal* (in international law) Māori version were prejudiced through denied rights (land and resource alienation, institutional racism, and powerlessness), without recourse to the courts of law. Rangatiratanga Māori was dismantled. As Stewart-Harawira (2005) argues:

> Indigenous educational historiographies provide readings of the sustained and deliberate attack on the collective nature of indigenous social and political structures in an attempt to absorb indigenous "remnants" into the relations of production that sustain Western capitalism, thus facilitating European access to the lands and resources needed for the expansion of the capital. (p. 16)

The 1987 *Lands Case* (see *New Zealand Māori Council v Attorney-General* [1987] 1 NZLR 641 at 668) however brought about a shift in attitude in one major respect—it brought about an acceptance of the two Treaty texts in law and developed some Treaty principles, partnership (creating responsibilities analogous to fiduciary duties) between Māori and the Crown, clarification around principles, and for many a renewed belief by Māori in the rule of law.

The Māori Language Act

Longstanding Māori activism and resistance to the colonialist onslaught eventually began to gain some traction, and in 1986 saw a landmark finding of the Waitangi Tribunal.[4] The response of the Tribunal to the Māori language claim that te reo Māori should have been protected was irrefutable. The Tribunal not only agreed that state policies had jeopardized the Māori language, in breach of the expectations in the Treaty, but went beyond that to allocate responsibility for widespread Māori educational "failure" as residing within the education system, concluding that:

> The education system in New Zealand is operating unsuccessfully because too many Māori children are not reaching an acceptable standard of education. For some reason they do not or cannot take advantage of it. Their language is not adequately protected and their scholastic achievements fall

far short of what they should be. The promises of the Treaty of Waitangi of equality in education as in all other human rights are undeniable. Judged by the system's own standards Māori children are not being successfully taught, and for that reason alone, quite apart from a duty to protect the Māori. (Waitangi Tribunal, 1986, pp. 58–59)

That same year, on July 20, 1987, the Māori Language Act declared te reo Māori an "official" language of New Zealand. It states: "Whereas in the Treaty of Waitangi the Crown confirmed and guaranteed to the Māori people, among other things, all their taonga: And whereas the Māori language is one such taonga ... The Māori language is hereby declared to be an official language of New Zealand" (Māori Language Act, 1987, p. 2). Te reo Māori is one of New Zealand's two official spoken and written languages. Its status, however, is yet to be recognized and reflected in practice in educational settings through the core curriculum in spite of its legal and political recognition.

The Treaty in Education

Imperialism, through its colonial outpost here in Aotearoa (Smith, 2012), was anchored in Aotearoa via the Treaty but, as has previously been argued, was swiftly dishonored (Mikaere, 2011; Mutu, 2010). Powerful mythologizing discourses then took hold (Ballara, 1986; Bevan-Smith, 2010, 2012). As Ballara (1986) succinctly put it, "In the end, in spite of the treaty, it was to be the concept of the wandering savage who had no rights to land that was adopted and recognized by the settler governments once self-government was attained" (p. 36). Educational pathways were mapped out *for* Māori in a context of contempt. The touchstone of whitestream education policy was established by Clarence Beeby in 1938, reflected in a statement prepared for Labour Prime Minister Peter Fraser, in which he wrote: "Every person, whatever his level of academic ability, whether he be rich or poor, whether he live in town or country, has a right, as a citizen, to a free education of the kind for which he is best fitted, and to the fullest extent of his powers" (Alcorn, 1999). It was the touchstone as education became free, secular, and compulsory, and with narrowly defined assimilatory aims for Māori it was little more than a factory conveyor belt to domesticated subservience as it was determined "he [Māori] was best fitted."

In recent years Māori have been positioned as a "priority" group throughout government policy (Ministry of Education, 2008, 2012). This is both nonsense and misleading. It is nonsense because it is mere rhetoric (nothing changes), and misleading because it hoodwinks both Māori and Pākehā into thinking that their appearance in policy fosters the idea that Māori, as a "priority group" are accorded special "privileges" when in fact the reality is Māori struggle for linguistic, social, cultural, and spiritual survival. The following section looks at how Kōhanga Reo have been captured systemically through discourses of "quality," evaluation, and review, and the exigencies of the regulatory framework. It overviews the steady decline of these centers first documented by Skerrett-White (2001), Skerrett (2010), and more recently in the findings of the Waitangi Tribunal (2012).

The rise and decline of Kōhanga Reo

The beginnings of the Kōhanga Reo movement as we know it was to stay the decline of te reo Māori and to address issues of socio-cultural disruption and concerns of identity loss (Skerrett-White, 2003). By bridging the sociolinguistic gap between the native older speaking generation and the younger generation/s some of the socio-cultural disruption associated with language loss would be alleviated whilst also contributing to a socio-culturally rejuvenated *iwi* (Māori people/tribes) Māori. In this respect Kōhanga Reo has been the leading light in terms of spearheading a bilingual/immersion stream of education in Aotearoa/New Zealand. It is a movement led by the people, for the people, in the Māori language. However, by its very nature Kōhanga Reo is swimming against the tide and constantly having to resist the hegemonic politics of capture as overviewed herein.

The chapter *The rise and decline of te koohanga reo: The impact of government policy* (Skerrett-White, 2001) overviewed its development in a context of rapid reform, centralized (State) controls, and neoliberal restructuring under the guise of "devolution." Further, in a presentation to the TKR National Trust Board in 2002, Skerrett stated:

> In terms of policy that supports whānau involvement and policy that supports the dual language, care and education roles—the gap is glaringly obvious—there in none. In fact public policy has been introduced which deliberately undermines the revernacularization goals of TKR—the subsidy cuts of the 1990s for a start, which took parents out of Kōhanga because you

had to be either in full-time employment or a full-time student in order to access the subsidy. One does not have to be brilliant to see how that policy would affect young Māori parents, especially in rural areas. (p. 19)

Within a very short time of the inception of TKR, the apparatus of the state proved to be antipathetic to what Kōhanga was trying to do-revitalize the Māori language at the unit of whānau (the smallest unit of Māori tribal structures). Skerrett-White (2001) argued, "This New Right or Neo-Conservative ideology is about the coupling of the neo-liberal views of 'individualism' with a traditional conservative view of 'power to the state'" (p. 12) and documented the subsuming of Māori aspirations in the "rush of reform" with the acquiescence of the TKR national representative body. Not much has changed. The following is a critique of policies that have impacted on TKR with, perhaps unintended, negative outcomes.

Policy documents—The Meade report

In 1988 ECE came fully under the Education Department (now the Ministry of Education). The Working Group Report (known as the Meade Report) (Meade, 1988) promised much in terms of equity across the ECE sector (quality provision, more parental choice, adequate funding) but did not translate into appropriate policy (see *Before Five*, 1988). The Meade Report noted the place of te reo Māori and tikanga Māori as concerns of Māoridom and as central tenets of quality ECE provision and the terms of reference included Treaty recognition. Skerrett-White (2001), however, argued that an unintended outcome of that Report was that it locked Kōhanga Reo settings into a pattern of decline and stated, "The writing was on the wall that TKR would not only be shifted to 'education' [portfolio], but that it would be subjected to the same educational reforms of marketization and regulation as other educational providers" (p. 14). In other words, TKR was to be subjected to a regulatory framework meant for the whitestream sector.

Before Five policy statement

The policy statement *Before Five*, issued in December 1988, by the government reneged on earlier promises of equity in the Meade Report. It opted for an independent reviewing regime, from an essentially "developmental" epistemological frame, as well as assuring a compliance regime in a regulatory structure (Waitangi Tribunal, 2012) from an English-oriented ontological frame. The developmental frame was based on the arbiters of "correct" or "normal" development and colonizing theories of child development. The ontological frame forced the TKR movement into compliance where Pākehā norms and behaviors became the benchmark.

Since the early heady days of Kōhanga Reo expansion from 1982 to 1992 when approximately 850 Kōhanga Reo came into being, the challenges for bilingual provision intensified. The glaringly obvious policy gaps have led to predictable outcomes. Of the shift of TKR from Māori Affairs to the Ministry of Education in 1989, it was argued: "While many working in the early childhood sector hailed the *Before Five* reforms, many working in TKR felt a sense of foreboding" (cited in Skerrett-White, 2001, p. 16). Early on in the establishment of TKR, Te Rangihau, a much esteemed Māori elder, warned:

> We have come a long way in a very short time with Te Koohanga[5] Reo and already I am seeing the signs of professionals in many fields homing in to take advantage of those aspects that can be documented for personal gain or for political purpose. If this trend was to continue and we were to take this to its extreme conclusion, my fear is that we would no longer have a people's movement, let alone a Maaori people's movement. (*Te TKR Trust Incorporated, 1984,* cited in Skerrett-White, 2001)

Wider *iwi* Māori (tribal groupings) were gravely concerned. Political developments in the intervening years have proven those concerns predictably well founded.

Pathways to the Future

In 2002 the government released its strategic plan *Pathways to the Future* (Ministry of Education, 2002). This strategic plan (written by the architect of the Meade Report and subsequent policy reform, Dr. Anne Meade) reiterated the content of the former Meade Report. It comprised three broad goals for ECE: the first focusing on participation and school preparation; the second on the quality of ECE; and the third on parental engagement in ECE services. Also supporting the attainment of these goals was the 2005 *Promoting Participation Project* (Ministry of Education, 2005), funding mechanism policy documents and subsequent Māori education policy and strategy documents (see Ministry of Education, 2008, 2009, 2012). They all reflect the same goals. None of them have made specific meaningful provision for ECE Māori language in bilingual immersion settings; all of them focus on teacher credentials for whitestream ECE teachers, participation in, and funding of whitestream educational settings.

The primary organizing structure under the strategic direction of *Pathways to the Future* for the ECE sector has been about boosting "quality," thus defined as being able to employ *professionally* educated teachers and increased parental choice, accompanied by a prescribed funding regime. "*Professionally* educated teachers" in this context is all about teacher qualifications (for the English sector) and their ability to design curriculum through their planning, implementation, and evaluation processes. That there was no national teacher education program in 2002 specifically designed for bilingual immersion settings meant a monopoly in ECE education at the time *Pathways to the Future* was developed. English-language teacher graduates were able to walk into paid employment while Māori-language teachers in bilingual immersion settings were not. Quality became synonymous with mainstream/whitestream (English) ECE concepts of quality and reflected in their hegemonic programs. Therefore the three broad goals in ECE education, as determined by the *Pathways to the Future* policy document, of *participation, quality,* and *parental engagement* translated to *participation* in "English-language" centers, *quality* equating to whitestream settings with (monolingual) English teachers; and *parental engagement* being about "choice" (to enrol in whitestream centers) meant the absence of any real choice for Māori who desired to send their children to Māori bilingual/immersion settings. They were forced into whitestream settings. This resulted in a rapidly declining Māori medium sector.

The impact of *Pathways* policy on bilingual/immersion settings

The Kōhanga Reo movement was swept away in the tsunami of strategic policy developed for an English-language sector, leaving a weakened "parent-led" or "whānau (family)-led" (TKR) movement and a reinforced teacher-led (monolingual English) sector. This created a "parent-led, teacher-led" divide. The divide was a policy divide that produced a breach of such proportions that one wonders if the Māori bilingual/immersion sector can ever fully recover. In a very real sense the divide created the moribund context for TKR (with a "non-quality" categorization under the *Pathways* policy) and a burgeoning mainstream ECE context (categorized as "quality" under the *Pathways* policy). Whilst the intention may have been noble, the professionalization of the teaching profession in the early childhood sector, the nascent Kōhanga Reo movement, was particularly vulnerable as there were no "officially sanctioned" teacher education programs. The two streams, whitestream and Māori bilingual/immersion, were then recalibrated and remunerated accordingly. Funding went the way of the professional "teachers." The Māori stream suffered losses in enrollments and a decline in funding. The follow-on inequities were cemented at the structural level and became evident in the practice, with accelerated growth in the English-medium sector and rapidly declining numbers and dwindling resources in the Māori-medium sector. The gross inequities are evident in 2013, with a declining Māori-medium sector (Waitangi Tribunal, 2012). While the Māori stream has been lodged in the linguafaction, the whitestream sector flourished.

Ka Hikitia Māori education strategies and *Tau Mai Te Reo*

The second (phase two) iteration of the Ka Hikitia strategy is *Ka Hikitia—Accelerating Success 2013–2017* (Ministry of Education, 2013a), a five-year strategy that covers early learning, and the primary, secondary, and tertiary education sectors. It asserts that it is the education system that needs to step up to ensure Māori students enjoy and achieve educational success, as Māori (p. 5). It acknowledges that immediate, rapid, and sustained change is needed. A central focus is the knowledge that "students do much better when education reflects their identity, language and culture" (p. 6). There are two underpinning critical factors for Māori to excel and reach their full potential. The first is quality provision and pedagogical leadership, supported by effective governance; the second is *iwi* (Māori) community (and business) engagement.

There are five guiding principles for the whole of the education sector:

1 *The Treaty of Waitangi–Ka Hikitia—Accelerating Success 2013–2017* gives expression to how the Treaty principles, particularly those of

partnership (creating responsibilities analogous to fiduciary duties) between Māori and the Crown, are applied in education. Ensuring Māori children and young people enjoy and achieve education success as Māori is a joint responsibility of the Crown and *iwi* Māori (Māori communities) to lift the performance of the education system.
2. *Māori potential approach—The Strategy* continues with the Māori potential approach that every Māori child can make a valuable social, cultural, and economic contribution to the well-being of their *whānau*, their community, and New Zealand as a whole, and achieve.
3. *Ako—a two-way teaching and learning process—*The notion of *ako* (teaching and learning) is grounded in the principle of reciprocity and the inseparability of student and *whānau*; educators' practices are informed by the latest research and are both deliberate and reflective.
4. *Identity, language and culture count—*Children and young people achieve when their identity, language, and culture are valued and included in teaching and learning in ways that support them.
5. *Productive partnerships—The Strategy* promotes a team effort. It requires everyone who plays a role in education to take action and work together. Productive partnerships are based on mutual respect, understanding, and shared aspirations, and are productive where there is an ongoing exchange of knowledge and information.

There are five focus areas: Māori language in education, early learning, primary and secondary education, tertiary education, and organizational success. For the purposes of this chapter I will be critiquing the first two. The first focus—Māori language in education—has as an outcome that all Māori students have access to high-quality Māori language education (p. 27). The Strategy states, "Māori language in education is critical for the Crown to meet its Treaty obligations to strengthen and protect the Māori language" (p. 28) and that "Effective Māori language educators have a high level of Māori language proficiency and are experts in second language acquisition" (p. 29). It suggests that *iwi* (Māori people/tribes) play vital roles in strengthening Māori language in education provision by providing supports, helping with Māori language in education teacher recruitment, providing professional development and *iwi*-specific curriculum, and ensuring Māori language is supported in the homes and marae. This focus area will be difficult to achieve in the absence of any plan as to how *iwi* Māori are supposed to provide these supports and involve themselves in such things as teacher recruitment, professional development, and curriculum development, especially when *iwi* Māori are so diverse, demographically thinned out, and many are living in colonized spaces. There is the added underlying assumption that *iwi* Māori (Māori people/tribes) have the infrastructure to be able to provide all these supports. Take, for example, my Ngāi Tahu *iwi*, which has moved into a post Treaty-settlement realm: it has one person employed by the Tribe to manage educational issues across most of the South Island. Whilst the strategy is aspirational, the provision of supports to meet this focus area is just not going to happen any time soon, without a realistic implementation plan and commitment of resource.

The second focus—early learning—states, "All Māori children participate in high quality early learning" (p. 31), and that "Strong early learning experiences provide critical foundations for success in later education" (p. 32). There is no reference under this focus area (pp. 31-32) to Māori language education in early learning. It does not come in until the two critical factors (quality and iwi engagement) are applied and even then the statements are somewhat vague. In terms of the quality provision critical factor it states, "*Te Whāriki*, the early childhood education curriculum, is an expression of biculturalism and provides a strong basis for teachers and leaders to promote aspects of Māori language and culture in early learning environments. *Te Whāriki* must be embedded within all services." (p. 33). However, it does not make the link between the first focus area that "all Māori students have access to high quality Māori language education" (p. 27) and the second focus area that "All Māori children participate in high quality early learning" (p. 31). A strategy designed to actually make a difference for all learners should start by blending the first two foci and state outright that "All learners have access to, and participate in, high quality Māori language early learning." That is, Māori language should be a part of the core curriculum in early years' education and beyond, for all learners. This has implications for all who want to be teachers in our country, and for initial teacher education. It gives expression to the idea below that it is the Māori language that is what defines us as a unique "kiwi" culture and identity.

Added to that, *Tau Mai Te Reo: The Māori Language in Education Strategy 2013-2017 Summary* (Ministry of Education, 2013b) (the language strategy that falls out of *Ka Hikitia: Accelerating Success 2013-2017*) states the Ministry of Education and its agencies, have obligations, as Crown agencies, to "actively protect Māori language as a taonga guaranteed under the Treaty of Waitangi" (p. 1), and that "Māori language in education is a defining feature of Aotearoa/New Zealand's education. The education system needs to create Māori language opportunities for all learners. For Māori language to flourish the language needs to be supported both within the education system and in communities" (p. 3); yet both strategies (*Ka Hikitia* and *Tau Mai Te Reo*) do not address the crux of the matter: the need to position the Māori language at the center of the curriculum alongside the English language across the whole education sector. Only 7.08 percent of the total Government expenditure on education is spent on Māori language in education (Ministry of Education, 2013b). One can extrapolate that it is a little over 92 percent that is spent on English language in education, regardless of whether it is literacy, numeracy, or ICT; if it is through the English medium then it is expenditure on the English language in education. To make a difference for all learners, Māori language must be officially mandated in the curriculum (as it is in law) alongside English (The Royal Society of New Zealand, 2013; Waite, 1992). *Tau Mai Te Reo* states, under Early Learning, that "By 2017 85 percent of ECE services reviewed by ERO will be working *to some extent or to a high extent* in partnership with Māori whānau" (p. 44, my emphasis added), but there is no visionary statement or expectation about the Māori language, knowledge, or worldviews.

Māori parents and grandparents were instrumental in establishing the Kōhanga Reo movement in the early 1980s, and subsequently its primary (elementary) school and secondary (high school) extensions. That is acknowledged in the current Ministry of Education strategies. But the sluggish response by the Crown to the Māori language educational needs of *whānau* Māori (Māori families) has seen the Waitangi Tribunal (2012) finding the Crown and its Ministry of Education in breach of its Treaty obligations (documented in detail in Chapter 3). The Māori medium sector in the early years has plummeted and is now in a state of steady decline. This has impacted on the whole stream of Māori-medium education. At this moment, the newly released Māori education strategy is talking about lengthening its stride and stepping up and simultaneously making demands on *iwi* Māori (Māori people/tribes), with no real plan or commitment of resource. Apart from the fact that the Crown has been ostensibly stepping up for the last 50 years, it appears to me to be a case of the Crown (and its administration) taking a giant step back. So my prediction for TKR, without radical systemic change and intelligent policy, is continued linguafaction (being the conditions within which language demise occurs) and a prolonged but perhaps inevitable language death. There are some basic fundamental steps that could be taken to provide some strong supports for the regeneration of the Māori language as a vernacular, but the Crown is still dragging the chain.

Conclusions

"A good idea goes nowhere if the system actually blocks it:
The litmus test for any country is the wellbeing of its families"
Nā Dame Iritana Tāwhiwhirangi, September 28, 2013

This chapter explores relevant policy documents impacting on Māori education in general (early years' bilingual/immersion education specifically), commencing with the colonial backdrop of Treaty signing and the treachery involved in turning it into an instrument of invasion and land alienation through the colonial courts. It overviewed the impact colonization and Treaty jurisprudence on Māori education generally and the Kōhanga Reo movement specifically. The succession of settler government legislative acts in a sequence of events largely determining land tenure, and socio-political structures (councils, hospitals, prisons, churches, asylums, and schools), meant the imposition of a foreign system as far as Māori were concerned. Political developments and public policies ushered in systematically undermined the Treaty as enforced assimilation was on the educational agenda for Māori. Māori rights went unprotected. Māori socio-cultural disruption is the result. Māori language shift occurred at the same rate as land loss. Māori resistance has been fine-tuned. Māori resurgence is inevitable.

Kōhanga Reo was established to stay the impact of language loss and socio-cultural dislocation experienced in Māori communities. The 1985–1986 legal decision concerning the recognition and role of te reo Māori (the Māori language) as a language of the state concluded that the Māori language could be regarded as a "taonga" (treasured possession) and therefore had a guaranteed right to protection under the terms of the Treaty of Waitangi (Waitangi Tribunal, 1986). This led to the Māori Language Act, 1987. But in spite of those legal and political developments our language and culture are still threatened. We Māori always have to adapt ourselves (our values, ways of being, and language) into a whitestream system that simply does not work. Whilst it may be true that no language can reside only within the early years or school system, it is widely acknowledged that the state education system, including Playcentre and Kindergarten, played a major role in bringing the Māori language to near death through the shift from Māori to English. All early childhood centers could therefore play a pivotal role in helping to reverse that language shift, but it is only the bilingual immersion centers that currently have success.

Whilst the principle of partnership of coming out of the *Lands Case* underpins the current Māori education and language strategies (see Ministry of Education, 2013a, 2013b), it has been identified that the partnership is problematic when it is controlled by the Crown. We have inherited a legacy of problematic partnership once the 1835 Declaration and Treaty were breached—practically on signing. That is why this section is concluded with the very insightful quote from the Kaihautū (leader at the helm) of the Kōhanga Reo movement and worthwhile repeating here: "A good idea goes nowhere if the system actually blocks it: The litmus test for any country is the wellbeing of its families" (Dame Iritana Tāwhiwhirangi, personal communication).

Aotearoa has been cloaked in the fabric of the coloniser, in spite of the warning that was given by Aperahama Taonui in 1840 at the signing of the Treaty of Waitangi, referred to at the outset of this chapter. Taonui put out a resounding warning not to lay a shroud on the Treaty of Waitangi, but to cloak the Treaty with our unique, kiwi-feathered, cloak from this place, Aotearoa. The warning was prophetic and solemn in its sense of foreboding. Kōhanga Reo has been shrouded, systematically divested of its unique and prized feathers. Still only partially state-funded it has been usurped as part of the Crown-regulated mainstream ECE sector (Waitangi Tribunal, 2010, 2012).

Our language is our life force; it nourishes our souls and feeds our minds. If we think of language as a taonga and a valued resource, then the growth of bilingual children will greatly enhance the nation's mana and wealth in a system in which both the official spoken and written languages are equally sanctioned, equally valued, equally loved, equally honored; as was envisioned in the Treaty of Waitangi and reflected in law. If we do not, then we pass up the most vitally significant way of unraveling and understanding the dominant discourses of myth-making. We have no other way of inversion—or turning things around. Our language is our last defense. It houses our stories, our worldviews, our knowledge/s; it is our cultural archive, our national treasure, and provides us with a place to stand—our tūrangawaewae.

Notes

1. Educational settings in Aotearoa are Crown entities or bodies established by law in which the Government has a controlling interest through regulation—but that are legally separate from the Crown.
2. Common law is derived from custom and judicial precedent or case law in contrast with statute law.
3. *R v Symonds* (1847), NZPCC 387.
4. A commission that has been established to examine Māori claims for restitution for breaches of the 1840 Tiriti o Waitangi.
5. Some tribal dialects prefer the written double vowel to a macron, as in Koohanga and Kōhanga.

References

Alcorn, N. (1999). *To the Fullest Extent of his Powers: C. E. Beeby's Life in Education*. Wellington, NZ: Victoria University Press.

Ballara, A. (1986). *Proud to be White? A Survey of pākehā prejudice in New Zealand*. Auckland, NZ: Heinemann Publishers.

Bevan-Smith, J. (2010, August/September). Making a meal out of mockery. In *Mana: The Māori News Magazine for all New Zealanders*, (95), 42–44.

Bevan-Smith, J. (2012). *The New Cannibal Club: Deconstructing History in Aotearoa New Zealand*. Unpublished doctoral thesis. University of Auckland, New Zealand.

Fishman, J. (1991). *Reversing Language Shift. Theoretical and Empirical Foundations of Assistance to Threatened Languages*. Clevedon: Multilingual Matters.

Kawharu, H. (2013). *Kawharu Translation (1975)*. Retrieved from www.waitangi tribunal.govt.nz/treaty/kawharutranslation.asp.

Māori Language Act, 1987. New Zealand Legislation. Retrieved from http://www.legislation.govt.nz/act/public/1987/0176/latest/DLM124116.html.

May, S. (2010). Curriculum and the education of cultural and linguistic minorities. In P. Peterson, E. Baker, & B. McGaw (Eds), *International Encyclopedia of Education* (Vol. 1, pp. 293–298). Oxford: Elsevier.

Meade, A. (1988). *Education to be More. Report of the Early Childhood Care and Education Working Group*. Government Printer, Wellington.

Mikaere, A. (2011). *Colonising Myths Māori Realities: He rukuruku whakaaro*. Wellington: Te Wānanga o Raukawa, Huia Publishers.

Ministry of Education. (1996). *Te Whāriki: he whāriki mātauranga mō ngā mokopuna o Aotearoa: Early Childhood Curriculum*. Wellington, NZ: Learning Media.

Ministry of Education. (2002). *Pathways to the Future: Nga huarahi arataki. A Ten Year Strategic Plan for Early Childhood Education*. Wellington: Ministry of Education.

Ministry of Education. (2005). *Review of Targeted Policies and Programmes: Ministry of Education Review of Promoting Early Childhood Education Participation Project*. Wellington: Ministry of Education.

Ministry of Education. (2008). *Ka hikitia—Managing for Success: Māori Education Strategy 2008-2012*. Wellington, NZ: Ministry of Education.

Ministry of Education. (2009). *Ngā haeata mātauranga: Annual Report on Māori Education, 2007/08*. Wellington, NZ: Ministry of Education.

Ministry of Education. (2012). *Me Kōrero—Let's Talk! Ka hikitia—Accelerating Success: 2013-2017*. Wellington, NZ: Ministry of Education.

Ministry of Education. (2013a). *Ka Hikitia: Accelerating Success 2013-2017: The Māori education strategy*. Wellington, NZ: Ministry of Education.

Ministry of Education. (2013b). *Tau mai te reo: The Māori Language in Education Strategy 2013-2017*. Wellington, NZ: Ministry of Education.

Mutu, M. (2010). Constitutional Intentions: The Treaty of Waitangi texts. In M. Mulholland & V. Tawhai (Eds), *Weeping Waters: The Treaty of Waitangi and Constitutional change*. Wellington: Huia Publishers.

New Zealand Māori Council v Attorney-General [1987] 1 NZLR 641 at 668.

Skerrett, M. (2010). A critique of the Best Evidence Synthesis with relevance for Māori leadership in education. *Journal of Educational Leadership, Policy and Practice*, 25(1), 42–50.

Skerrett-White, M. N. (2001). The rise and decline of te kohanga reo: The impact of government policy. In J. Ritchie, A. Parsonson, T. Karetu, N. Te Uira, & G. Lanning (Eds), *Te Taarere aa Tawhaki* (pp. 11–22). Hamilton: Waikato University College.

Skerrett-White, M. N. (2003). *Kia mate rā anō a tama-nui-te-rā: reversing language shift in kōhanga reo*. Unpublished doctoral thesis. Te Whare Wānanga o Waikato, University of Waikato, Hamilton.

Smith, L. (2012). *Decolonizing Methodologies: Research and Indigenous Peoples* (2nd ed.). NY: Zed Books Ltd.

Stewart-Harawira, M. (2005). *The New Imperial Order*. Wellington, NZ: Huia Publishers.

The 1835 Declaration of Independence. (2013). *New Zealand History Online*. Retrieved from www.nzhistory.net.nz/media/interactive/the-declaration-of-independence.

The Royal Society of New Zealand. (2013). *Languages in Aotearoa New Zealand*. Wellington, NZ: The Royal Society of New Zealand.

Waitangi Tribunal. (1986). *Te Reo Māori Report*. Wellington: GP Publications: Waitangi Tribunal.

Waitangi Tribunal. (2010). *Pre-publication Waitangi Tribunal Report 262: Te Reo Maori*. Wellington, New Zealand Waitangi Tribunal.

Waitangi Tribunal. (2012). *Pre-publication Waitangi Tribunal Report 2336: Matua Rautia: The Report on the Kōhanga Reo Claim*. Wellington, New Zealand Waitangi Tribunal.

Waite, J. (1992). *Aoteareo: Speaking for Ourselves*. Wellington, New Zealand: Learning Media.

Webb, D., Sanders, K., & Scott, P. (2010). *The New Zealand Legal System: Structures and Processes* (5th ed.). Wellington: Lexis Nexis NZ Limited.

3
Crown Breaches, Neoliberal Reforms, and Radical Pedagogy

Mere Skerrett

Abstract: *This chapter overviews bilingual/immersion education, Crown breaches and offers a radical pedagogy through Māori immersion early childhood care and education (ECCE). It asserts that in order for the Māori language to be a working living language in communities across Aotearoa then it needs to be fully incorporated into the education system. It presents an extended analysis of recent and relevant Waitangi Tribunal Reports demonstrating how the Crown and its administration (the Ministry of Education) has reneged on its fiduciary responsibilities and duties under the Treaty of Waitangi through its policies and procedures. This has led to a weakened Māori immersion ECCE infrastructure and decreasing options for Māori parents and children. It is an imperative that the Māori language supports in ECCE are strengthened.*

Ritchie J., and M. Skerrett. *Early Childhood Education in Aotearoa New Zealand: History, Pedagogy, and Liberation.* New York: Palgrave Macmillan, 2014.
DOI: 10.1057/9781137375797.0007.

> Ko te reo te Mauri o mana Māori
> (Nā Sir James Hēnare, Waitangi Tribunal, 1985)
> The language is the core of our Māori culture and mana.
> The language is the life force of the mana Māori

Introduction

This chapter provides a deeper analysis of the Waitangi Tribunal Reports of 2010 and 2012 with regard to the Treaty breaches in education. The critique is largely concerned with the parent-led/teacher-led divide that was created with *Pathways to the Future* (Ministry of Education, 2002). It is asserted that the injustices that had been hardwired into the New Zealand education system through the colonial arrangements are ongoing. However, the findings of the Tribunal are of such magnitude that they cannot be ignored. The Waitangi Tribunal (2012) raised issues of funding inequities, enrollment drop offs, an irregular regulatory framework, and the overall deleterious effects on Māori bilingual/immersion education. It is reasserted in this chapter that te reo Māori needs to be fully incorporated into the education system. That is, it needs to be a compulsory part of the curriculum in exactly the same way that English is. After all, it is an official language. This has profound implications for initial teacher education (ITE) in this country. The nature of Māori language proficiency that ITE providers expect of graduating teachers is affected by a very wide range of socio-political, historical, and linguistic factors, and influenced by the policy environment. However, the policy environment lags behind the bilingual immersion field. In line with the *Ka Hikitia* strategy, ITE needs to step up to meet the development needs of a full education system in a bilingual/bicultural context. This requires consistent and large resources focused on it and to Māori language advancement in ITE. Only then will the system produce sufficient number of graduating teachers with the level/s and range/s of Māori language proficiency needed for full, high-quality teaching of the curriculum in bilingual/immersion early years education and beyond. Following on from a rendering of the Treaty breaches, a pedagogy of vigilance is imperative to counter the reach of the neoliberal agenda in education. This will assist with resisting the coercion of teachers into compliance regimes that are harmful to teaching and learning, damaging to teacher/learner relationships, and ultimately dismantle democratic ideals.

Waitangi Tribunal reports

The Waitangi Tribunal (2012) report documents how Kōhanga Reo (TKR), wanting to raise quality by employing additional qualified staff (according to the Kōhanga Reo determination of what counts as "qualified"), struggled under the structural inequities. The system "failed to cover the extra cost [of employing credentialed staff] as it did for teacher-led ECE centers ... [which was] an unacceptable limitation built into the structure of the Crown's funding regime" (p. 232). The non-recognition of the qualification mandated by the TKR National Trust Board as a teaching qualification (Te Tohu Whakapakari), as found by the Waitangi Tribunal, effectively blocked TKR from accessing teacher-led rates (p. 53).

Funding inequities

The rapidly changing policy environment in early years' education was all about "professionalizing" the teaching profession. Hegemonic "quality" discourses were flavor of the day, eventually becoming tightly linked to funding. The Tribunal argued that the Crown funding regime simply did not provide equity with the funding available to other parts of the ECE sector and that, in any event, Kōhanga Reo should be able to advance their own determinants of "quality." It also argued that Kōhanga Reo should *not* be *compelled* to adopt the Crown's measures for assessing and improving quality for other ECE services, simply to achieve parity in funding (p. 331). As first argued by Skerrett-White (2001) and later by the Waitangi Tribunal (2010, 2012), the inequitable parent-led/teacher-led divide in ECCE (see Chapter 2) resulted in a steady decline of Kōhanga Reo who were, and still are, the major providers of bilingual immersion education in the ECE sector. That puts the whole Māori stream of education at risk. *Pathways to the Future* (Ministry of Education, 2002) was the policy document that created the divide, perhaps inadvertently so. Rather than creating parallel pathways for the Māori stream, it collapsed the sectors into one pathway (ruled by whitestream definitions of policy), essentially inhibiting the Māori stream or Māori immersion pathway. This phenomenon is endemic in colonial systems where one pathway ends up being validated and legitimated; the other sits outside the system. The error is that if the measure of "quality" was the extent to which whitestream ECE centers were meeting the rights of *all* children in Aotearoa to a bilingual-bicultural education, then in fact whitestream funding would cease. It is only the Māori-medium part of the sector that is currently meeting this "quality" measure. Kōhanga Reo has been successful in creating Māori/English bilingual speakers (MEBS). Such success has been well documented (see Ministry of Education, 2013b; United Nations Educational, Scientific and Cultural Organization Report, 2010). The UN Educational, Scientific and Cultural Organization Report (2010) describes how the Kōhanga Reo movement demonstrates what a powerful force indigenous language revitalization can be, not only for education but also for social cohesion. Monolingual English settings produce monolingual monocultural children, totally out of step with *Te Whāriki*. It is asserted here that a definer of "quality" in concert with *Te Whāriki* has to be the extent to which a center promotes MEBS and biculturalism in Aotearoa/New Zealand, bilingualism being the first step to entry into a pluralistic society. Hornberger (2008) provides further ideological clarification around this issue particularly in terms of bilingual education and its relationship to multilingual/multicultural education. She argues that at its best it is:

1 multilingual in that it uses and values *more than one* language in teaching and learning;
2 intercultural in that it recognizes and values understanding and dialogue across diverse lived experiences and cultural worldviews; and education that draws out the knowledge/s students bring to the educational setting.

Hornberger clearly positions bilingual education on the multilingual continuum. She also legitimates and validates the heritage knowledge/s and language/s that are located in communities and how they can be brought into the educational setting through bilingual/immersion programs. Heritage/majority language bilingualism provides an awareness of self (and thus a determination of self) and also of others: other culture/s, values, and meta-ways of thinking and knowing.

Declining enrollments for Kōhanga Reo

The Waitangi Tribunal (2012, p. 28) traced the pattern of declining enrollments, which paralleled declining centers through closures. After the expansionary momentum of the 1980s when the number of Kōhanga Reo rose by an average of 80 per year to reach 809 Kōhanga (with 14,514 enrollments—nearly half of all Māori enrollments in ECE) in 1993, it then slowed, abruptly flattened, and declined steadily to 586 Kōhanga, with a roll of 9,808 in 2001. This marked a decline of 181 Kōhanga Reo and 4,494 enrollments over a very short space of time—just five years (p. 28). Currently there are 463 Kōhanga Reo catering to 9,631 learners (Ministry of Education, 2013b). The Tribunal also found that the Crown's failures to address the place of Kōhanga Reo has led to actions and omissions inconsistent with the principles of the Treaty of Waitangi, 1840, namely "the principles of: partnership; the guarantee of rangatiratanga; the obligations on the Crown to make efficient and effective policy and to actively protect te reo Māori in ECE through TKR; and the principle of equity" (p. xvii).

Tribunal findings of Crown Treaty breaches

The recent Waitangi Tribunal (2012) findings are that there has been serious prejudice to the TKR movement as a result of Crown (and its Ministry of Education) Treaty breaches. In particular these have been:

- *inadequate recognition in ECE policy for TKR;*
- *a decline in the proportion of Māori participating in TKR;*
- *adverse impacts on the reputation of the TKR movement;*
- *serious underfunding of the Trust for services provided and insufficient funding to TKR, which has led to a decrease in capital expenditure posing a relicensing risk and exposing 3,000 mokopuna (young learners) to the possibility of losing their* Kōhanga Reo *buildings*
- *imposition of a regulatory regime including licensing criteria that has paid insufficient regard to the particular TKR environment; and*
- *an ERO evaluation methodology that remains focused on teacher-led models unbalanced against the important results that TKR provide for te reo transmission and whānau development (p. 335).*

Curriculum implications

Te Whāriki (Ministry of Education, 1996) has failed to make a difference with respect to Māori language advancement in the whitestream of early years' education. One only has to go into centers throughout New Zealand to witness that and read the Education Review Office[1] reports. It is touted as being New Zealand's first bicultural curriculum document. The Foreword written by the Acting Secretary for Education, Lyall Perris, states:

> This is the first bicultural curriculum statement developed in New Zealand. It contains curriculum specifically for Māori immersion services in early childhood education and establishes, throughout the document as a whole, the bicultural nature of curriculum for all early childhood services. (p. 7)

Yet the relationship between biculturalism and bilingualism is not grappled with, and nor are the implications for teaching and learning in a bicultural context. There has been scant professional development facilitating teacher access to the Māori text in *Te Whāriki*, many believing the Māori text is a translation of the English text. It is not. From an Indigenous Māori perspective, *Te Whāriki* is still in an immature state, still in the nest. It has not yet begun to flex its wings.

Section 7(a) of The Māori Language Act, 1987 directed Te Taura Whiri i te Reo Māori to pursue strategies designed to give effect to the declaration of te reo Māori as an (the) official language (Waite, 1992). The ultimate goal of such policy was equal status to both te reo Māori and English at the official level. Therefore, Māori is an official language *de jure (according to law, by right, legally)* and English is an official language *de facto (existing in fact whether officially recognized or not)*. Aotearoa is thus a bilingual country (officially) and all efforts should proceed toward promoting its bilingualism and biculturalism (Waite, 1992; The Royal Society of New Zealand, 2013). However, in practice, in whitestream educational settings, it is the de facto English language that is the default setting and the language of provision, in spite of the stated intentions of *Te Whāriki* to establish the first ever bicultural curriculum.

Teacher education

Teacher shortages for bilingual immersion settings have long been an issue. The Waitangi Tribunal (2010) Report quoted newspaper headings: "*Call for boost in Māori teacher tally*" (Press, July 11, 2007), "*Bilingual teachers in hot demand*" (Sunday Star Times, August 4, 2002), "*Demand at all levels for bilingual Māori teachers*" (Evening Post, January 30, 1997), "*Teacher crisis jeopardises bilingual classes*" (Dominion Sunday Times,

September 30, 1990), "*High personal cost for kura kaupapa principals*" (Kia Hiwa Ra, November 1996). The Waitangi Tribunal (2010, 2012) found that what was striking about Māori-medium surveys was the apparent gulf between the numbers of parents who wanted their children in Māori-medium education, and the number of children actually attending, showing demand far outweighed supply in terms of numbers of teachers and settings thus limiting participation. The Tribunal findings stated:

> There have also been various initiatives to attract and retain te reo and Māori-medium teachers, and to increase Māori-language teaching resources ... But what is striking about surveys is the apparent gulf between the numbers of parents who wanted their children in Māori-medium education, and the number of children actually in that form of learning. Surveys showed the demand for Māori-medium education was much higher than the rate of participation. This, along with the shortage of Māori-speaking teachers, suggests that supply could not keep up with demand. Thousands of Māori children (there is no need to be more precise than that) were in monolingual English education when their caregivers wanted either Māori-immersion education or (principally) bilingual education including Māori.... the gap between supply and demand would have been so large that it was impossible to meet that demand to a reasonable standard within a reasonable time. Officials needed to have taken proper and rigorous steps in the early 1980s to estimate kōhanga demand. Had they done so, it seems likely that they could have foreseen the massive uptake of kōhanga reo through the 1980s and into the next decade, and inevitably an equally large flow-through demand for Māori-medium primary education ... Indeed, a report commissioned by the (then) Department of education in 1987 estimated (conservatively, as it turns out) that at least 1,000 more Māori speaking teachers would be needed over the following decade to service the kōhanga generation. (2010, pp. 11–12)

Māori had no other option but to put their children into monolingual English educational settings because of the attrition in the bilingual/immersion settings, instead of the much needed expansion to cater for the demands.

Regulatory framework

The inappropriateness of the neoliberal regulatory framework (one-size-fits-all) was borne out by the Waitangi Tribunal (2012), which found: "Rather, there needs to be greater partnership and cooperation in formulating regulations and licensing criteria specific to the needs and situation of TKR" (p. 293). Failure to enact a meaningful partnership has meant that the TKR National Trust body has, perhaps inadvertently, certainly unintentionally, acted as the Trojan horse of hostile policy. The strategic focus of the last decade has resulted in funding inequities, leading to operation shortfalls. This strategic focus has directly affected the ability of Māori immersion (bilingual) settings to stay afloat in what has become a very competitive, increasingly privatized, market place for ECE. The promotion of "parental choice," narrow colonial prescriptions of "quality," and poor engagement with the Māori language communities in terms of educating parents and caregivers regarding the benefits of bilingual immersion education has reduced options for Māori parents wanting Māori immersion, in spite of the rhetoric. This has been the direct cause of attrition of enrollments in Kōhanga Reo and their closures.

Neoliberal reforms

Neoliberal advancements in the context of globalization mean the system is always restructuring or reterritorializing itself, which, for Māori, and importantly Māori language, make it difficult to establish secure ground, to respond to the ongoing linguafaction, let alone respond to the ever increasing reach of neoliberal reforms. The parent-led/teacher-led divide perpetuated injustices in the allocation of resources right in the nascent phase of the Kōhanga Reo movement. This forced Kōhanga Reo into having to respond to a market-driven pedagogy instead of stabilizing and expanding the kaupapa-driven pedagogy. Recently I presented what I called *The Politics of Pedagogical Darwinism* (Skerrett, 2013) based on the chapter by Henry A. Giroux (2012b) called *Can Democratic Education Survive in a Neoliberal Society?* where he argued:

> If teachers are truly concerned about how education operates as a **crucial site of power** in the modern world, they will have to take more seriously how pedagogy functions on local and global levels to secure and challenge the ways in which power is deployed, affirmed, and resisted within and outside traditional discourses and cultural spheres. (p. 11)

I challenged the teachers to adopt a "pedagogy of vigilance." My provocation was that if teachers are truly concerned about making a difference in children's lives, truly concerned about children's agency, about children's power to take control over their own learning, about teaching and learning as a democratic right, about promoting MEBS, then teachers must learn how to resist the external controls that *coerce* them into becoming technicians, not educators; that force them into compliance and domestication, not liberation. Teachers now, more than ever before, need to exert their powers of critical thinking, of alertness, of political nous. As Paolo Freire (1972) once argued, teaching is a highly political act. I also want to refer another chapter titled *The Disappearance of Public Intellectuals* (Giroux, 2012a), because of how these chapters, set in a global context, reveal with clarity the neoliberal context with relevance to Aotearoa/New Zealand, and the reforms felt not only in the universities but also in schools and the early childhood centers.

The first of these chapters deals with the Politics of Economic Darwinism (inspiring my title—*The Politics of Pedagogical Darwinism*) transposing economics into a pedagogical frame, with implications for the practice. Economic Darwinism, according to Giroux (2012a), is the situation where economics drives politics, transforming citizens into consumers, society into a stock exchange, where long-term societal investments are de-railed and replaced by short-term profits, and where compassion and concern for others are viewed as a weakness. Just take for example the past 150 years of long-term investments into our infrastructure, and the contemporary short-term pawning off of State Owned Enterprises, where lands, seas, waterways, and airways are all up for grabs, including hospitals, parks and prisons, airports, postal, telephone and power companies, educational settings, and so on—once part of the public system, they are now subject to being disassembled and privatized. Giroux (2012b) argues that as the language of privatization, deregulation, and commodification replaces the discourse of the "public good," all things public (including public schools—particularly public schools—which are hugely important sites), other crucial infrastructures, and public services are viewed either as a drain on the market or as a pathology, and systematically divested or privatized. Individual prosperity becomes the greatest of social achievements.

Moreover, Giroux (2012c) asserts that vulnerable populations once protected by the state are now considered a *liability* because they are viewed as either flawed consumers or present a threat to the politics of the right. They constitute a form of *human waste* and are considered disposable (with human pipelines going direct to the chain gangs of labor [or jails] to support the private estate) because they are thought of as, "unworthy of sharing in the rights, benefits, and protections of a substantive democracy" (Giroux, 2012a). The new politics of disposability and the competitive culture of capitalistic greed represent more than an economic crisis, but speak to a deeply rooted crisis in education, and social justice. Economic Darwinism drives the political context of education and educational policy, not only turning people into consuming machines but converting children into stocks, human capital, disposable units. The question remains—*Is education about processing people, or is it a people process?*

Giroux (2012a) also argued that we are witnessing the "disappearance of critical intellectuals and the collapse of those public spheres which offer a sense of *critical* agency and social imagination." In other words we are becoming global clones or puppets to the neoliberal puppeteers. The frame for public education is this corporate-based ideology that embraces standardized curriculum (and associated measures or standardized assessments); top-down governing structures (and their associated hierarchical arrangements that devalue family and community); courses that promote entrepreneurial values (with an almost fanatical focus on technology, literacy, and numeracy); and the reduction of professions to job training sites.

The corporate model displays a deep disdain for the ideals of humanizing education and well-being, but instead is entirely related to the market place and the production of human capital. This poses a direct threat to democracy. Giroux (2012a) talks about Edward Said—saying that:

> Before his untimely death, Edward Said, himself an exemplary public intellectual, urged his colleagues in the academy to directly confront those social hardships that disfigure contemporary society and pose a serious threat to the promise of democracy. He urged them to assume the role of public intellectuals, wakeful and mindful of their responsibilities to bear testimony to human suffering and the pedagogical possibilities at work in educating students [children] to be autonomous, self-reflective, and socially responsible. Said rejected the notion of a market-driven pedagogy, one that created cheerful robots and legitimated organized recklessness and illegal legalities. (p. 2)

In opposition to such a pedagogy of recklessness (creating clones and puppets), Said argued for what he called a "pedagogy of wakefulness" and its related concern with the politics of *critical engagement*. That is ever important—critical engagement. It is through critical pedagogy that the human brain is neurologically awakened and transformation is the platform, not domestication.

Let us return to the debate about critical theory, critical engagement, and theories of change. At the heart of Māori language education (what many of us call Kaupapa Māori praxis) is the pedagogy of critical engagement for transformation. A failure to understand this fundamental principle of Kaupapa Māori praxis runs the risk of retrenchment to a pedagogy of domestication, a pedagogy of hierarchy (complete with sovereigns and slaves), and a pedagogy of Darwinian thinking. Do we want to domesticate our children—or educate them? This is a critical question. Critical because we now have new limits opening up with new horizons, new possibilities of experience—daily! We are in a constant state of flux, and, dare I say it, crisis. We have to cultivate resilience and the courage to face the risks in times of crisis—and often in the face of adversity.

We Māori know only too well what it is like to sit, to live, on the horizons of an enigmatic future, where our language and concepts are on the brink, and yet embrace a radical hope for the future of our tamariki (children). We cling to a pedagogy of hope when we actively promote our language and center Māori worldviews. As we celebrate the new horizons of our world through Matariki,[2] we prepare to celebrate what we have, what we might imagine, and our freedom to discourse the world I turn here to such a radical pedagogy through alternative speak.

Radical (critical) Kaupapa Māori pedagogy

I turn now to storytelling as pedagogy drawing on discourses around Rūaumoko/Rūaimoko, our earthmother's unborn child. Robyn Kahukiwa's book *Taniwha* (Kahukiwa, 1986) helped to shape a junior elementary school classroom project around Papatūānuku and her unborn child, Rūaimoko. This project was carried out with 14 young children around six years of age. Robyn Kahukiwa is a great storyteller (and artist) who is able to draw from our Māori worldviews and represent these via literature for ongoing storytelling. The ongoing storytelling and translation through art, re-storying, song, and drama then becomes experience for those who actively engaged. They emerge with renewed insights and understandings. In this way her story becomes their story so to speak, in that it becomes their shared experience. This story book became an important part of the classroom project around Papatūānuku, our earthmother, and her unborn child (responsible for earthquakes) because of the ongoing earthquakes we have experienced in Christchurch over the last three years. To briefly background the children involved in this project—not all are speakers of Māori. Many are just beginning the journey into "te reo." There is a mix of Māori language abilities, with only a few children having some fluency, but with the emergent speakers when there are world-view shifts they are acutely apparent in their conversations as they juxtapose world views. Kahukiwa's book forms the basis of a video clip—and underpinned the project. The video clip and song became an absolute favorite within the classroom; the lyrics speak of the creation of land through rupture, through the ebb and flow of movements, through life and death. During this project the teacher noticed a little girl digging out in the grounds. When the teacher asked what the little girl was doing she replied, "I am digging down to Rūaimoko—I can see Rūaimoko's skin." In further discussion with a *whānau* (family) member, another child was going to dig down to talk to Rūaimoko and when his Mum asked, "How are you going to talk to Rūaumoko?" He said, "You get a big big spade and dig o all the way down." Mum said, "That would take quite a long time wouldn't it?" The child responded, "Ok—I've got another idea—we'll get a microphone and put that down there [to have a conversation with Ruaimoko]."

The project transformed discourses, views, and the physical space of the classroom. This is an example of *critical* literacy—because it is connected to children's lives, their experiences, and their ways of thinking about them in a new becoming—a demonstration of storytelling provoking a shift in awareness, increasing the intelligible link to children's affective domains and responses—from the tremor (and terror) of earthquakes to the sanctity and renewed respect (and searching) for Rūaumoko:

▸ of storytelling facilitating critical discussion,
▸ of children and teacher and community in dialogue,
▸ of children's exploration and problem solving,
▸ of children's stories through their creations,
▸ of the feminization of phenomena, healing, and sanctity.

Therein lies my provocation: how do we maintain the sanctity of a radical pedagogy for social justice; for what ethically we know to be a right for all of our children: to be free thinkers; to be embracing of life at the horizon with the surety of their own agency? How we do that within Darwinistic pedagogies?

The development of critical literacy

Critical literacy frameworks are active processes in the co-construction of knowledge. One cannot understand messages without acting on them either internally (by thinking about them) or externally (doing something about them). Descriptive acts are domesticating. It is what children think and do that shifts the teaching learning nexus to a critical frame, where interpretative analysis represents the internalized action of text (the thinking about text). So a critical literacy act is internalized action (the thought) into external agency (the action) during the co-construction of knowledge in real meaningful contexts. As children engage with text, through their discussions, questions, and answers, their understandings are deepened. This is about children and adults actively engaging with one another in a deepening understanding of the symbols that flood young children's worlds. In the dominant hierarchical (teacher in control) approach to education of Indigenous children they have been coerced into taking on board the dominant view point of who they are. That process is dehumanizing. In creative literacy acts when children actively voice their own experiences, views, thinking, desires, likes, and dislikes they are voicing their own realities and shaping their own identities. It is this process that can present as a challenge to the unequal power relations as alternative perspectives and ways of operating are activated. The Rūaimoko project was just that, a critical literacy act. It is this storytelling through our treasured Māori language that the tamariki/mokopuna (children and grandchildren) can access the archive of Māori Indigenous world views.

Conclusions

That the Waitangi Tribunal (2012) Report found the New Zealand Ministry of Education in breach was not surprising to many of us involved in the Kōhanga Reo movement. It is a common theme of this book that the imperialistic imperatives of colonization disrupt the histories, stories, and lives of Indigenous peoples. Imperialism is an ongoing project and as Linda Smith puts it, it still hurts, it is destructive, and it is constantly reforming itself. It is constantly territorializing. So the latest 2012 Tribunal findings are nothing new. I restate we Māori are all the time trying to fit a white-frame that simply does not work. We must continue the struggle to work within our Māori Indigenous frames of reference. That is we must take control of what is ours, our tino *rangatiratanga*. I have argued elsewhere that *tino rangatiratanga* is all the more important because of globalization and its neoliberal reforms, as it is an ability to critically mediate the way the world enters into our minds, bodies, and daily lives; that is, to make sense and meaning of the world at the individual level and at the cultural level, and reconciled from a position that is Māori. It is self-identification and definition at the personal level and self-determination culturally. It is an ability to think critically and respond collectively in order to mediate external influences and the rate of change that impacts upon our lives and resources (Skerrett-White, 2003).

The chapter *The Rise and Decline of te Kōhanga Reo: The Impact of Government Policy* (Skerrett-White, 2001) overviews the rapid expansion of the TKR movement within its first ten years of establishment. Māori leaders proposed that *iwi* Māori should start teaching the very young to bridge the language gap between the ageing native-speaking elders and the very young that had occurred as a result of colonization and the subtractive assimilatory policies of the education sector. The excitement of those times in hearing young children speaking te reo Māori further galvanized the Māori people into action and fuelled the movement, building on that early success. However, that rapid expansion was short-lived. In just under a decade the movement was shifted to the "education" portfolio and fully into the whitestream system. It was like our Māori stream was polluted when subjected to a host of educational reform and regulation that compromised its sustainability. That was predictable and predicted by many working in the Kōhanga Reo field. The *Ka Hikitia* strategy, which is meant to be about the system stepping up, continues to take giant leaps backward. That said, the urgency around a collaborative teacher/*iwi* Māori commitment to making a difference, to adopting a pedagogy of vigilance, provides us all with a radical hope for the future. Through kaupapa Māori pedagogy it is argued that the Māori Indigenous narratives, ways of thinking and being, disrupt and unravel the dominant discourses that seek to domesticate children. They trouble the myths. They release the trauma of cognitive dissonance. Counter-colonial discourses through renarrativization provide the critique to dehegemonize the system. They help to resist and critique the myth making that has shrouded our cultural archive. It was argued that the success of Kōhanga Reo and the whole of the Māori-medium sector provide the evidence of the powerful force indigenous language revitalization is. Therefore the incorporation of te reo Māori fully into the core curriculum is the next step up for the system. Until that happens, the Crown through its administration will continue to be in Treaty breach mode.

Notes

1. The Education Review Office is an independent government department that reviews the performance of schools and early childhood services, and reports publicly on what it finds.
2. Matariki is the rising of a cluster of tiny stars and is a celestial signal of the beginning of the Māori New Year.

References

Durie, M. (2001). *A Framework for Considering Māori Educational Advancement.* Opening address. Hui taumata mātauranga, Taupo, New Zealand.

Durie, M. (2003). *Māori Educational Advancement: At the Interface Between te ao Māori and te ao whanui.* Hui taumata mātauranga tuatoru, Taupo, New Zealand.

Freire, P. (1972). *Pedagogy of the Oppressed.* Penguin.

Giroux, H. A. (2012a). The disappearance of public intellectuals. *Truthout.* http://www.counterpunch.org/2012/10/08/the-disappearance-of-public-intellectuals/ (accessed June 11, 2013).

Giroux, H. A. (2012b). Can democratic education survive in a neoliberal society? *Truthout.* http://truth-out.org/opinion/item/12126-can-democratic-education-survive-in-a-neoliberal-society (accessed June 11, 2013).

Giroux, H. A. (2012c). Gated intellectuals and ignorance in political life: Toward a borderless pedagogy in the Occupy Movement. *Truthout.* http://truth-out.org/opinion/item/8009-gated-intellectuals-and-ignorance-in-political-life-toward-a-borderless-pedagogy-in-the-occupy-movement (accessed June 16, 2013).

Hornberger, N. (2008). *Multilingual Education Policy and Practice: Ten Certainties (grounded in indigenous experience).* Retrieved January 1, 2010, from http://www.gse.upenn.edu/~hornberg/

Kahukiwa, R. (1986). *Taniwha.* Auckland, New Zealand: Puffin Books.

Māori Language Act, 1987. New Zealand Legislation. Retrieved from http://www.legislation.govt.nz/act/public/1987/0176/latest/DLM124116.html.

Ministry of Education. (1996). *Te Whāriki: he whāriki mātauranga mō ngā mokopuna o Aotearoa: Early Childhood Curriculum.* Wellington, NZ: Learning Media.

Ministry of Education. (2002). *Pathways to the Future: nga huarahi arataki. A Ten Year Strategic Plan for Early Childhood Education.* Wellington: Ministry of Education.
Ministry of Education. (2012). *Me Kōrero—Let's talk! Ka hikitia—Accelerating Success: 2013–2017.* Wellington, NZ: Ministry of Education.
Ministry of Education. (2013a). *Ka Hikitia: Accelerating Success 2013–2017: The Māori Education Strategy.* Wellington, NZ: Ministry of Education.
Ministry of Education. (2013b). *Tau mai te reo: The Māori Language in Education Strategy 2013–2017.* Wellington, NZ: Ministry of Education.
Rika, M. (2012). *Whitiora.* Moonlight Sounds.
Skerrett, M. (2010). A critique of the best evidence synthesis with relevance for Māori leadership in education. *Journal of Educational Leadership, Policy and Practice, 25*(1), 42–50.
Skerrett, M. (2013). *The Politics of Pedagogical Darwinism.* Unpublished Conference Presentation: Christchurch, New Zealand: The Gathering, June 15, 2013.
Skerrett-White, M. N. (2001). *The Rise and Decline of te kohanga reo: The Impact of Government Policy.* In J. Ritchie, A. Parsonson, T. Karetu, N. Te Uira, & G. Lanning (Eds), *Te Taarere aa Tawhaki*, (pp. 11–22). Hamilton: Waikato University College.
Skerrett-White, M. N. (2003). *Kia mate rā anō a tama-nui-te-rā: Reversing Language Shift in kōhanga reo.* Unpublished doctoral thesis. Te Whare Wānanga o Waikato, University of Waikato, Hamilton.
The Royal Society of New Zealand. (2013). *Languages in Aotearoa New Zealand.* Wellington, NZ: The Royal Society of New Zealand.
United Nations Educational, Scientific and Cultural Organization. (2010). Reaching the marginalized. Retrieved February 1, 2010, from http://www.unesco.org/en/efareport/reports/2010-marginalization/
Waitangi Tribunal. (2010). *Pre-publication Waitangi Tribunal Report 262: Te Reo Māori.* Wellington, New Zealand Waitangi Tribunal.
Waitangi Tribunal. (2012). *Pre-publication Waitangi Tribunal Report 2336: Matua Rautia: The Report on the kōhanga Reo Claim.* Wellington, New Zealand Waitangi Tribunal.
Waite, J. (1992). *Aoteareo: Speaking for Ourselves.* Wellington, New Zealand: Learning Media.

Part B
Indigenizing "Whitestream" Early Childhood Care and Education Practice in Aotearoa

4
Contextual Explorations of Māori within "Whitestream" Early Childhood Education in Aotearoa New Zealand

Jenny Ritchie

Abstract: *This chapter provides a historical overview of whitestream (see Skerrett, this volume) provision of early childhood care and education (ECCE) services within Aotearoa, positioning this within the wider socio-cultural/ political contexts of colonization and assimilatory policies. The origins of the various early childhood services are explained as emerging from needs identified in New Zealand communities at particular periods, with long-standing colonialist ideology re-emerging as deficit discourses, with assimilation of Māori into the whitestream being the underlying intention, despite the aspirations of both the 1840 Tiriti o Waitangi and 1996 early childhood curriculum Te Whāriki espousing bicultural possibilities whereby Māori maintain the right to uphold te ao Māori values (Māori worldview), traditions, and language, whist also accessing the knowledges of the Western world.*

Ritchie J., and M. Skerrett. *Early Childhood Education in Aotearoa New Zealand: History, Pedagogy, and Liberation.* New York: Palgrave Macmillan, 2014.
DOI: 10.1057/9781137375797.0008.

Introduction

In this chapter, the growth of ECCE services in Aotearoa New Zealand, with a particular focus on inclusion/exclusion of Māori children and families, will be positioned within historical and international contexts. Colonization by Great Britain, legitimized in 1840 with the signing of Te Tiriti o Waitangi/The Treaty of Waitangi, was one of the furthest and latest extensions of international imperialism, toward the end of an era when the strongest European countries had competed for global wealth, resources, and prestige. Consistent with its history as a former British colony, this small Pacific nation aligns itself with larger Western countries such as Britain, Australia, Canada (British Commonwealth ties), and more recently the United States of America, with its political economy an extension of global imperialism/capitalism. The impacts of colonization are not only historical but ongoing, as Māori continue to suffer the impacts of low socioeconomic status and poor educational outcomes (Ministry of Health, 2006). Māori children are particularly vulnerable to these (Policy Strategy and Research Group Department of Corrections, 2007). This chapter briefly traverses the history of early childhood services in Aotearoa, drawing upon the work of Helen May (2009, 2013). This has been characterized by being a series of diverse "flax-roots" movements, emergent and responsive to the contexts of their time of origin. Weaving through the discourses of empire and colonization have been filaments of egalitarianism contrasting with twisted threads of white superiority, underpinning justification of the disenfranchisement and marginalization of Māori within their own country. In this chapter, I consider ways in which ethical visions of hope may have opened up lines of flight, a process in which the visionary leadership and advocacy of certain key people have been hugely influential in inspiring ethical relationality and practices (Rose & Novas, 2005). Connections will be made to a Deleuzian-inspired "everyday and immanent practice" of ethics that might enable us to "begin to identify what is good and what is bad for us as well as for others, or what conjoins us with, or separates us from a life" (Frichot, 2007, p. 178). Rather than viewing Māori as passive victims of colonization, the view is that all parties have taken responsibility for their engagement, since, in a Deleuzian view, "each self has a primary responsibility to cultivate and practice an attitude of relation to others that enables the emergence of ethical social forms" (Bignall, 2007, p. 208).

Promises, promises: *Te Tiriti* and *Te Whāriki* as ethical visions

Historian James Belich has written that stories of European imperialism are "dramatic and traumatic, etched deep into the psyches of both victors and victims" (Belich, 2009, p. 22). The juggernaut of colonization reached these remote Pacific islands quite late in comparison to many other parts of the globe. This timing is significant, because it meant that by the time the British seriously contemplated colonizing these islands, anti-slavery human rights discourses were beginning to change the way the colonizers could treat the colonized. Furthermore, Māori were proactively and astutely entrepreneurial in their relationships with settlers (King, 2003). This opened up trajectories of possibility that may not have been as apparent in previous colonization endeavors elsewhere.

The 1840 Tiriti o Waitangi/Treaty of Waitangi (Orange, 1987), and the 1996 early childhood curriculum, *Te Whāriki: He whāriki mātauranga mō ngā mokopuna o Aotearoa* (New Zealand Ministry of Education, 1996), are both documents that are symbolic of an ethical relationship between the Indigenous Māori and the non-Indigenous settler/Pākehā citizens of Aotearoa New Zealand. Both documents can be viewed as containing an ethical vision as a source of hope, the realization of which remains, in both contexts (national and ECCE), largely unrealized. Yet in many ways, the field of early childhood has been a site of endeavor toward realization of the ethical promise of recognition of the Indigenous people, their language, values, and ways of being, knowing, and doing.

Settler assumption of sovereignty

Early Western observers had noted with shock the 'indulgent' way in which Māori treated their children (Belich, 1996; Salmond, 1991). Once the missionaries arrived in 1814, Māori were repelled by the brutality demonstrated toward children in mission schools (Walker, 2004). The 1835 Declaration of Independence, in which Māori proclaimed their own sovereignty, was a strong statement of Māori autonomy, and was gazetted internationally by Great Britain. This led directly to the need in 1840 for Britain to legitimate the inevitable settlement of its entrepreneurial citizens, resulting in the signing of *Te Tiriti o Waitangi*/The Treaty of Waitangi by Britain and a large number of Māori chiefs. This treaty was unusual in its recognition of Māori rights to their chieftainship, lands, "*taonga*" (all things of value to them), and to be British citizens with recognition of equality of belief systems (Orange, 1987). This then, was an ethical vision for a country in which Māori, the Indigenous peoples, would live alongside the British settlers, each party respectful of the rights and responsibilities of the other.

The rapid assumption of sovereignty by the British settlers, who established their own government in 1852, and the onslaught of British emigration, coupled with the deaths of many Māori mainly as the result of introduced diseases to which they were not immune, quickly led to the situation by the mid-1850s, of Māori becoming a minority in their own country. Having assumed sovereignty and formed their independent parliamentary system, which initially excluded then later marginalized Māori, the settlers proceeded to pass myriad legislation and regulations that disenfranchised Māori from their lands, and also from their rights to their own cultural practices and language. Ignoring the undertakings contained within Te Tiriti o Waitangi that should have protected Māori independence, successive settler governments perpetrated an agenda that determined an assimilative process that would ultimately destroy parallel Māori institutions (Ballara, 1986; Orange, 1987; Walker, 2004). This was despite ongoing Māori resilience and resistance, such as was demonstrated in their response to the use of physical punishment in schools, as related by Henry Taylor, an Inspector of Native Schools in 1862:

> Corporal punishments and an over-rigid discipline have done much to drive away many children from the schools. A punishment which to us would appear by no means harsh, would to a Native seem cruel and excessive. As Native parents never inflict chastisement upon an offending child, our summary mode of dealing with young delinquents must seem strange and tyrannical. It would not be unwise in future to pay some little deference to their feelings in this subject. An ineffective Teacher is soon detected by a Native, and in this respect their perception is more acute than that of a European; when once a Teacher's inability is detected, his prestige is lost, and the school is consequently injured". (Henry Taylor, as cited in New Zealand Parliament, 1862, p. 35)

Taylor further recognized that both Māori collectivism and the Māori language were oppositional forces to the settler colonization project that was to be imposed through schooling. In addition to their collectivist society:

The Native language is also another obstacle in the way of civilisation, so long as it exists there is a barrier to the free and unrestrained intercourse which ought to exist between the two races, it shuts out the less civilised portion of the population from the benefits which intercourse with the more enlightened would confer. The school-room alone has power to break down this partition between the two races. (Henry Taylor, as cited in New Zealand Parliament, 1862, p. 35)

These excerpts from reports to Parliament in 1862 are telling in their frank disregard for *te ao* Māori (the Māori world), symbolic of the colonial project, and the desire of the colonization machine to systematically dismantle the fabric of Māori ways of knowing, being, and doing.

Progressive traditions

The new immigrants of settler societies bring with them to their new land their hopes and dreams for their future and a better life for their children and descendants. An ethic of egalitarianism was a strong feature of settler discourse in New Zealand: "The working class call no man master—indeed, they are all the working class—it is no uncommon thing to see a judge ploughing, or a general peeling potatoes" (as cited in Belich, 2009, p. 157). The 1877 Education Act established state-funded, secular primary schooling for all children from age five. Early New Zealand kindergartens, however, were initiated by philanthropists, and had religious and Froebellian influences (May, 1997, 2006). In 1893 New Zealand was the first country in the world to grant women the right to vote. In the 1930s there was "a mood of idealism" (Beeby, 1992, p. 90), a strong current of progressivism flowed through the country. Influenced by the democratic ideals of John Dewey, Maria Montessori, and others, shared through the international New Education Foundation/Fellowship movement, the hopes for education as a force for societal transformation "were extravagantly high" (Beeby, 1992, p. 90). This was an era when "When faith in the power of education, properly understood, was so widespread and so strong" (Beeby, 1992, p. 90). After the Great Depression of the 1930s, the Labour Government introduced the ethical innovation of a system of universal "social welfare" that aimed to support members of the national community from the "cradle to the grave," promoting a sense of community responsibility (Lunt, 2008). In 1935 an alliance was formed between Wiremu Tahupotiki Ratana, head of a Māori political movement, and Michael Joseph Savage, leader of the Labour Government, in which Savage signaled the commitment of his party to attend to Māori concerns "in accordance with the spirit of the Treaty of Waitangi" and to Māori well-being (Savage, as cited in Walker, 2004, p. 185). Despite these espoused good intentions, racism was pervasive and discrimination against Māori persisted (Baker, 2012).

"Flax-roots" early childhood education and care services

The beginnings of ECCE services in Aotearoa are sometimes described as having "flax-roots," as having emerged in response to urgent needs identified by local communities. Māori were "early acquisitors" of schooling provision provided by missionaries from 1816 onward (May, 1997, p. 20). Initially this provision was through the medium of *te reo* Māori (the Māori language), but with the signing of Te Tiriti o Waitangi came an immediate assumption of colonizer sovereignty, with English-medium schooling a key tool of assimilatory colonization. Diminishment of *rangatiratanga* (self-determination) was tightly implicated in the loss of language, lands, and the capacity to uphold *mana* (authority, prestige) through careful management of resources. Distinct tribal and sub-tribal authority was eroded in a deluge of legislation and regulation. The great white/Anglo settler tidal wave (Belich, 2009) of breaches of articles of the Treaty, whose intentions if sustained by the Crown, would not only have protected Māori authority, language, lands, and belief systems, but should also have upheld Māori as having equal status to the settlers. The impacts on Māori were severe, with Māori communities decimated by illness and dislocation.

By the early 1900s, Māori infant mortality had become a huge concern of Māori leaders such as Te Puea Hērangi, a leader of the Tainui tribe who cared for large numbers of Māori children orphaned by a series of influenza epidemics; Sir Maui Pomare, a medical doctor who became Minister of Health in 1901; and Sir Apirana Ngata, a lawyer who became Minister of Native Affairs in 1928. The vast majority of Māori, who remained predominately located in rural areas, did not get access to the health services available in the urban settlements. Nor did they feature in the beginnings of ECCE and care services, which had emerged in the major townships, initially in response to outcry at "baby farming" of infants from illegitimate relationships and destitute families. The names of Māori children are not evident on the rolls from early kindergartens because of this rural/urban separation of Māori and settlers (May, 1997). The Playcentre movement began during World War Two, and was initially a middle-class *Pākehā* (of European ancestry) parent cooperative organization advocating a "free-play" philosophy (May, 2001). Post war, Māori, urged to seek a "better life," were increasingly lured into the cities to serve in industries. This did not necessarily mean relinquishing their language and cultural values and practices, although unfortunately this was the over-whelming result for many. Sir Apirana Ngata wrote an autograph, which appears in the opening pages of the New Zealand early childhood curriculum, Te Whāriki:

> E tipu e rea
> Mō ngā rā o tōu ao
> Ko tō ringa ki ngā rākau a te Pākehā
> Hei ara mō tō tinana
> Ko tō ngākau ki ngā taonga a ō tīpuna Māori
> Hei tikitiki mō tō māhunga
> Ko tō wairua ki tō Atua
> Nāna nei ngā mea katoa. (Sir Apirana Ngata, 1949, as cited in New Zealand Ministry of Education, 1996, p. 3)

Here is a translation:

> Grow up and thrive for the days destined to you.
> Your hand to the tools of the Pākehā to provide physical sustenance.
> Your heart to the treasures of your Māori ancestors as a crown for your brow.
> Your soul to your God, to whom all things belong.
> (Brougham & Reed, 1999, p. 89, as cited in Mahuika, 2008, p. 12)

Māori retained the aspiration, as expressed in *Te Tiriti o Waitangi*, that they might uphold their *rangatiratanga* (self-determination), retaining their language and values, whilst participating and benefiting in the offerings from the wider Western world (Skerrett, 2007). Yet once they began to participate in ECCE settings run by *Pākehā*, this proved to be a challenge.

Māori pre-schools

Prior to 1960, very few Māori children were enrolled in early childhood settings in Aotearoa, although no particular records were kept

(McDonald, 1973). In 1960 a government-commissioned social policy document known as "the Hunn Report" (Hunn, 1960) listed a range of concerns regarding Māori health, education, housing, crime-rate, land ownership, and employment, all of which remain current areas of disparity (Dale, O'Brien, & St. John, 2011; Ministry of Health, 2006). It recommended a new policy of social "integration" for Māori, which involved "combining, not fusing, the Māori and Pākehā elements to form one nation in which Māori will remain distinct" (The Hunn Report, 1961, p. 61). Whilst exposing Māori educational "failure," the report appeared to be laying the blame on Māori, not on an education system that had consistently failed to meet the needs of Māori. It imported from overseas the negative, victim-blaming perspectives of "cultural deprivation" and "deficit," which saw "minority" children as having inadequate language, a shortage of concepts, lack of life experiences, poor motivation, and an inability to deal with the abstract, and attributed these failings to the child's upbringing (Metge, 1990, p. 23). Parental apathy was considered to be responsible for Māori children's failure (Walker, 2004). Yet the report also identified the need for the Ministry of Māori Affairs to "do something" about the educational difficulties faced by Māori children in the education system (McDonald, 1973). This led to the establishment in 1962 of the Māori Education Foundation, which, in line with progressive thinking, internationally recognized "pre-school education" as an "agency of social reconstruction" (McDonald, 1973, p. 1). The founding chairperson stated that:

> Our main objective is clear: to strengthen Māori home life and the language, general knowledge and experience of children in their crucial pre-school years until every Māori child is as well-equipped as the European child to come to school (McLaren, 1974, p. 87).

Although still defining Māori aspirations in *Pākehā* (Western) terms of educational success, the focus on the early years of life was supported by the Māori Women's Welfare League, which began actively promoting the benefits of ECCE for Māori children. By 1968, 472 pre-school centers for Māori families had been established, mainly in rural areas of the North Island, following the Pākehā model of Playcentre, which involved cooperatives of mothers offering play-based sessional programs. Geraldine McDonald's 1973 study of "Māori Mothers and Pre-school Education" involved 103 mothers in 12 rural, marae-based, and urban services. McDonald found that despite the mothers espousing a strong desire to preserve the Māori language, this was actively occurring in only two of the settings. There appeared to be no appreciation yet of the potential for ECCE services to be an ideal vehicle for this purpose, although in some of the settings Māori mothers were using *te reo* Māori (Māori language) informally (McDonald, 1973). Cultural practices being maintained within the pre-schools included: *karakia* (grace) being said before meals; respect for *whakapapa* (Māori ancestry) being instilled within the marae-based pre-schools; *manaakitanga* (generosity and hospitality) demonstrated through practices such as daily sharing of *kai* (food) at meal-times and through *powhiri* (welcoming) for guests; intergenerational connection being maintained through regular involvement of grandmothers; and Māori songs and crafts featuring as part of the programs. McDonald criticized those who had blamed poor Māori achievement on Māori attitudes and lack of motivation, saying that "if it is values that have to change, it has to be the dominant culture's negative stereotyping of Māoris" (McDonald, 1973, p. 175). Her research indicated that early childhood programs run by Māori for Māori were most successful for Māori, developing Māori women's leadership skills, expressing Māori values and culture, and networking well within the Māori community. She considered Māori leadership to be particularly necessary in communities in Māori/Pākehā settings in order to retain Māori involvement and uphold *te reo* and *tikanga* Māori (Māori language and culture).

Chance to be equal

Perhaps as a reaction to the upsurge in civil rights movements, the 1970s saw increasing international emphasis on theories of cultural deprivation, positioning "minorities" in "deficit." In 1972, a New Zealand Department of Education publication, "Māori Children and the Teacher," stated that Māori children's "vocabulary is particularly inadequate when they want to express ideas" (1972, p. 42). Deficit discourses were part of a "race pathology" circulated through the colonization project internationally via Social Darwinist and Eugenicist race ideologies manifest in mechanisms such as IQ tests and the prejudices and low expectations of teachers (Harris, 2008; Simon, 1996).

The idea that ECCE might provide Māori children with an opportunity to "equalize" their educational achievement was picked up by another ECCE research project, based at the Centre for Māori Studies and Research at the

University of Waikato and led by my mother, now Emeritus Professor Jane Ritchie. Influenced by the USA Headstart model, the project ran from 1974 to 1976, and involved 36 families who lived in the urban setting of Hamilton, in the North Island. Of these families, only six parents spoke Māori, and none spoke Māori regularly to their children. Some grandparents also spoke Māori, but English was the first language for all but one of the children who attended the early childhood center, which had been named Te Kohanga by Tainui tribal leader Sir Robert Mahuta. Although English was the dominant language in the homes, "Māori cultural values and attitudes prevailed in the preschool families" (Jane Ritchie, 1978, p. 22). This was reflected in their regular enjoyment of traditional foods such as *hāngi* (feast cooked in an earth oven), frequent attendance at *tangihanga* (funerals), and trips to the coast to gather *kaimoana* (seafood). Ritchie pointed out the working-class positionality of these Māori families, who whilst located away from their home *marae* (village, meeting place), maintained these links despite lack of car ownership. They were not engaged in kindergartens and were unavailable to do the obligatory "mother-help" days at Playcentres.

Despite its recognition and support for Māori cultural identity and values, the project was couched in the deficit language of the day. Jane Ritchie wrote that, "A child who has never been to a beach,[1] or to a farm, is in fact deprived of developing language around these experiences, and it these contexts that children's books frequently utilise" (1978, p. 23). The project had a strong focus on providing a regular format of educational, particularly language-oriented activities and had been criticized for this teacher-directed "structure" by proponents of "free play." In introductory comments in the book by both W. L. Renwick, then Director-General of Education, and prominent progressive educationalist Jack Shallcrass, both were quick to defend the project's deliberate focus of providing about one-third of each pre-school session in teacher-directed activities, whilst the other two-thirds were free play. Jane Ritchie, a psychologist whose doctoral work had been on Māori childrearing, and Nancy Gerrand, an experienced new entrant primary school teacher, collaborated in developing the program for the pre-school. It featured a heavy emphasis on reading picture books to and with children. The three features of their book program were frequent repetition of favorite stories in the opening session of the morning program and discussion thereof; a daily small group story reading session; and the daily "home-book" program where each child chose a book to take home to be shared with her or his family overnight. Despite his critique of "compensatory education" in general,

Shallcrass recognized the dedicated, individualized focus of the educational program provided by Te Kohanga:

> No child was lost or left behind: each was cherished and every little step in learning was nurtured. We need more such defined and specific attempts to probe and develop individual possibilities. As each child moved ahead on his or her own track that progression was celebrated, acknowledged, recorded and enhanced. Thus as disadvantage was overcome, by and with each child, the record showed it. Everyone knew it: everyone could be prouder for it and rejoice in it. (Shallcrass, 1978, p. xvi)

Despite the socioeconomic marginalization of the Māori families who were involved in this project, their commitment to the program and to their children's education was evident in the full attendance, "loyalty, support and enthusiasm" demonstrated by both *tamariki* (children) and *whānau* (families) (Jane Ritchie, 1978, p. 133).

Repositioning te Ao Māori as central to education

The 1970s is sometimes described as an era of Māori "renaissance," notwithstanding that Māori had since 1840 continually and consistently agitated for recognition of what had been promised in *Te Tiriti o Waitangi*. Māori educators now began to have an influence within the state education discourse. The 1970 National Advisory Committee on Māori Education (NACME) report (1970) was a turning point in that at last, Māori were being consulted on Māori education policy. The report stated that teachers of Māori children should have "a sound working knowledge of the cultural background of Māori children" and that therefore teacher education programs "should provide for an understanding of contemporary Māori society including some study of Māori values and attitudes, and introduction to the language needs of Māori children, and methods of dealing with these as well as a background of the cultural and social history of the Māori" (NACME, 1970, pp. 8–9). The report was radical in its implication that in order to ensure that Māori children were equipped to reach their full potential, there was a need modify the system, not the children (Metge, 1990). This would require change by *Pākehā* (of European ancestry) teachers to take responsibility for understanding and including Māori language and culture. Significant also in this decade was the introduction by Māori academic Ranginui Walker of the concept of "biculturalism" into education discourse when, in 1973 (as cited in Simon, 1989), he identified that Māori children were immersed in two cultural codes, juxtaposing this alongside the monoculturalism of their Pākehā teachers (as cited in Simon, 1989, p. 27), thus subtly positioning these teachers, rather than their Māori pupils, as being in "deficit."

In concession to Māori demands, official education discourse began in the 1980s to advocate for the insertion of "Taha Māori" (a Māori dimension) into the curriculum alongside "multicultural education," which emphasized "cultural diversity" (Simon, 1989, pp. 23–28). Māori educators condemned this approach as exploiting Māori culture, which primarily benefited the Pākehā "mainstream." Graham Smith questioned the advisability of Pākehā gaining un-moderated access to Māori knowledge, and expressed concerns about the counter-productive effects resulting when monocultural Pākehā teachers were ill-equipped to deliver Māori content with any authenticity (G. H. Smith, 1990). Ranginui Walker (1985) identified Pākehā racism as a contributing factor to the undermining of the official "Taha Māori" policy by these teachers, and questioned the depth of official commitment to the policy in the light of the unwillingness to specify a time allocation for the teaching of taha Māori (Māori dimension). Judith Simon (1989) critiqued these education policies as designed to contain the resistance of Māori and other ethnic groups, in order to preserve the relations of dominance and avoid Māori calls for power-sharing, whilst maintaining a pretext of a discourse of egalitarianism.

In 1985 the country's early childhood services, previously divided into childcare (under the Department of Social Welfare), kindergarten, and Playcentre (under the Department of Education) and ngā Kōhanga Reo (under the Department of Māori Affairs) were brought together as "early childhood care and education" under the administration of the Department of Education. Early childhood teacher education now became integrated for all early childhood services, taught as a three-year diploma-level qualification. This was an internationally innovative and progressive step, validating the roles and status of early childhood workers and the important work of our sector (May, 2001).

Long-standing Māori activism and resistance to the colonialist onslaught eventually began to gain some traction. 1986 saw a landmark finding of the Waitangi Tribunal, a commission that has been established to examine Māori claims for restitution for breaches of the 1840 Tiriti o Waitangi. In their response to a claim by Māori that their language should have been protected, the Tribunal not only agreed that state policies had jeopardized the Māori language in breach of the expectations in the Treaty, but went beyond that to allocate responsibility for the widespread Māori educational "failure" as residing within the education system, concluding that:

> The education system in New Zealand is operating unsuccessfully because too many Māori children are not reaching an acceptable standard of education. For some reason they do not or cannot take advantage of it. Their language is not adequately protected and their scholastic achievements fall far short of what they should be. The promises of the Treaty of Waitangi of equality in education as in all other human rights are undeniable. Judged by the system's own standards Māori children are not being successfully taught, and for that reason alone, quite apart from a duty to protect the Māori language, the education system is being operated in breach of the Treaty. (Waitangi Tribunal, 1986, pp. 58–59)

A Māori teacher had informed the Tribunal of her view that:

> The frustrations of being a Māori language teacher are just the same as those of being a Māori in New Zealand society. The frustrations of being a Māori language teacher are essentially summed up in the feeling that the education system has invited you to be a mourner at the tangihanga (funeral) of your culture, your language and yourself. (Maika Marks, as cited in the Waitangi Tribunal, 1986, p. 57)

During the 1980s, Māori actively reasserted their rangatiratanga (authority) in relation to ECCE provision offered by Māori, for Māori, in the medium of Māori language, as Mere Skerrett has explained in Chapter 3.

New right enmeshment with liberal social policies

The "Fourth Labour Government" (1984–1989) has been described as an interesting mix of "New-Right individualism and collectivist interventionism" in service of equity (Middleton, 1992, p. 318). In 1988, the Labour Prime Minister and Minister for Education, David Lange commissioned a report on ECCE (Meade, 1988) that included the incorporation of *te reo* Māori and *tikanga* Māori (Māori language and culture) in its list of characteristics of "good quality" ECCE. This report then informed the government's new ECCE policy, "Before Five" (Lange, 1988). Prime Minister David Lange stated that, "This Government sees early childhood education as having a priority among its social policies" (as cited in May, 2002, p. 6). In line with that government's social policy agenda, The "Before Five" policy required that national guidelines to be drawn up for ECE were to take account of The Treaty of Waitangi. The Treaty/*Tiriti* had officially entered the ECCE discourse. During the late 1980s and early 1990s, diverse groupings within the ECCE sector separately publicly acknowledged a commitment to the Treaty of Waitangi (Ritchie, 2002).

However, in 1990, a National Government came to power, taking to further extremes the neoliberal privatization agenda introduced by its predecessor, but with scant regard for any social protections. Public money was diverted into private ECCE centers through government subsidies, with little accountability, enabling these services to retain significant amounts of profit (May, as cited in EducateNZ—Education News, 2005, p. 1). Schools and early childhood centers were now expected "to compete amongst themselves" within the "education market," parents and children were "recast as education consumers," and "the fetish of parental choice became predominant" (George, 2008, p. 17). In 1991, the Minister of Education, Lockwood Smith removed the requirement for school charters to address equity, equality of opportunity, and the Treaty of Waitangi, claiming this change would allow schools more "freedom" to be "flexible" to respond to community "choice" (McKinley, 1994; L. Smith, 1991). Neoliberal individualism thus displaced a commitment to an ethic of social equity and to recognition of the Indigenous people. As Hickey-Moody and Malins explain, "What capitalism deterritorializes on the one hand, it reterritorializes on the other" (Hickey-Moody & Malins, 2007, p. 15). The opportunities for *Tiriti*-aligned educational possibilities that had been opened up through the initial neoliberal reforms of the education system under Labour, were immediately shut down by the new National government:

> Lines of flight decode and deterritorialize, but can be—and always eventually are—recaptured or reterritorialized in molar processes such as institutionalized and bureaucratic educational practices that translate the desire of bodies into the line segments necessary to make 'education' happen. (Albrecht-Crane & Daryl Slack, 2007, p. 104)

Note

1 It should be noted that many Māori children in the 1970s (and today) visit the sea-shore reasonably frequently with their families, to gather *kaimoana* (traditional seafoods). Judith Simon (1996) has pointed out the tendency for Pākehā teachers to be unable to recognize and therefore validate the kinds of knowledges that Māori children had, since the teachers themselves were ignorant of these—for example, the knowledge related to attending *tangihanga* (Māori funerals) or gathering *kaimoana* (seafood).

References

Albrecht-Crane, C., & Daryl Slack, J. (2007). Toward a pedagogy of affect. In A. Hickey-Moody & P. Malins (Eds), *Deleuzian Encounters. Studies in Contemporary Social Issues* (pp. 99–110). Houndmills, Basingstoke, Hampshire, and New York: Palgrave Macmillan.

Baker, M. (2012). *Family Welfare: Welfare, Work and Families, 1918–1945.* Wellington: Te Ara—Encyclopedia of New Zealand. Retrieved from http://www.teara.govt.nz/en/family-welfare/page-3.

Ballara, A. (1986). *Proud to be White? A Survey of Pakeha Prejudice in New Zealand.* Auckland: Heinemann.

Beeby, C. E. (1992). *The Biography of an Idea: Beeby on Education.* Wellington: New Zealand Council for Educational Research.

Belich, J. (1996). *Making Peoples. A History of the New Zealanders from Polynesian Settlement to the End of the Nineteenth Century.* Auckland: Penguin.

Belich, J. (2009). *Replenishing the Earth: The Settler Revolution and the Rise of the Anglo-World, 1783–1939.* Oxford: Oxford University Press.

Bignall, S. (2007). Indigenous peoples and a Deleuzian theory of practice. In A. Hickey-Moody & P. Malins (Eds), *Deleuzian Encounters. Studies in Contemporary Social Issues* (pp. 197–211). Houndmills, Basingstoke, Hampshire, and New York: Palgrave Macmillan.

Dale, M. C., O'Brien, M., & St. John, S. (2011). *Left Further Behind.* Auckland: Child Poverty Action Group. Retrieved from http://www.cpag.org.nz/assets/Publications/LFBDec2011.pdf.

EducateNZ—Education News. (2005). Early Childhood Agreement Good For Children And Teachers.

Frichot, H. (2007). Holey space and the smooth striated body of the refugee. In A. Hickey-Moody & P. Malins (Eds), *Deleuzian Encounters: Studies in Contemporary Social Issues* (pp. 169–180). Houndmills, Basingstoke, Hampshire, and New York: Palgrave Macmillan.

George. (2008). The pursuit of profit in education—The penetration of business into the early childhood and primary schooling sectors. *New Zealand Journal of Teachers' Work, 5*(1), 13–20. Retrieved from http://www.teacherswork.ac.nz/journal/volume15_issue11.php.

Harris, F. (2008). Critical engagement with the deficit construction of Maori children as learners in the education system. *Critical Literacy: Theories and Practices, 2*(1), 43–59. Retrieved from http://criticalliteracy.freehostia.com/index.php?journal=criticalliteracy&page=issue&op=view&path[]=41&path[]=showToc.

Hickey-Moody, A., & Malins, P. (2007). Introduction: Gilles Deleuze and four movements in social thought. In A. Hickey-Moody & P. Malins (Eds.), *Deleuzian Encounters: Studies in Contemporary Social Issues* (pp. 1–24). Houndmills, Basingstoke, Hampshire, and New York: Palgrave Macmillan.

Hunn, J. K. (1960). *Report on Department of Maori Affairs*. Wellington: Public Service Commission.

The Hunn Report. (1961). *Te Ao Hou, 34*(March), 59–61. Retrieved from http://teaohou.natlib.govt.nz/journals/teaohou/issue/Mao34TeA/c28.html.

King, M. (2003). *The Penguin History of New Zealand*. Auckland: Penguin.

Lange, D. (1988). *Before Five: Early Childhood Care and Education in New Zealand*. Wellington: Department of Education.

Lunt, N. (2008). From welfare state to social development: winning the war of words in New Zealand. *Social Policy & Society, 7*(4), 405–428.

Mahuika, R. (2008). Kaupapa Māori theory is critical and anti-colonial. *MAI Review, 3*, 1–16. Retrieved from http://review.mai.ac.nz/index.php/MR/issue/view/11.

May, H. (1997). *The Discovery of Early Childhood*. Auckland: Bridget Williams Books, Auckland University Press.

May, H. (2001). *Politics in the Playground: The World of Early Childhood in Postwar New Zealand*. Wellington: Bridget Williams Books and New Zealand Council for Educational Research.

May, H. (2002). Early childhood care and education in Aotearoa—New Zealand: An overview of history, policy and curriculum. *Paper for*

Publication in *McGill Journal of Education*, Retrieved from http://www.aeufederal.org.au/Ec/HMayspeech.pdf.

May, H. (2006). 'Being Froebelian': An antipodean analysis of the history of advocacy and early childhood. *History of Education, 35*(2), 245–262.

May, H. (2009). *Politics in the Playground: The World of Early Childhood in New Zealand* (2nd ed.). Dunedin: Otago University Press.

May, H. (2013). *The Discovery of Early Childhood* (2nd ed.). Wellington: NZCER Press.

McDonald, G. (1973). *Maori Mothers and Pre-school Education*. Wellington: New Zealand Council for Educational Research.

McKinley, E. (1994). *Equity and Curriculum Policy in Aotearoa New Zealand: Challenges, Opportunities, Uncertainties*. Paper presented at the Australian Association of Research in Education Conference, University of Newcastle, 27 November–1 December 1994. Retrieved from http://www.aare.edu.au/94pap/mckie94285.txt.

McLaren, I. (1974). *Education in a Small Democracy—New Zealand*. London: Routledge & Kegan Paul.

Meade, A. (1988). *Education to be More: Report of the Early Childhood Care and Education Group*. Wellington: Government Printer.

Metge, J. (1990). *Te Kohao o Te Ngira, Culture and Learning*. Wellington: Learning Media.

Middleton, S. (1992). Equity, equality, and biculturalism in the restructuring of New Zealand schools: a life-history approach. *Harvard Educational Review, 62*(3), 301–322.

Ministry of Health. (2006). Decades of Disparity III: ethnic and socioeconomic inequalities in mortality, New Zealand 1988–1999. *Public Health Intelligence Occasional Bulletin Number 31*. Wellington: Ministry of Health and University of Otago. Retrieved from http://www.moh.govt.nz/notebook/nbbooks.nsf/0/37a7abb191191fb9cc256dda00064211/$FILE/EthnicMortalityTrends.pdf.

National Advisory Committee on Māori Education. (1970). *Māori Education*. Wellington: Department of Education.

New Zealand Department of Education. (1972). *Māori Children and the Teacher*. Wellington: School Publications Branch.

New Zealand Ministry of Education. (1996). *Te Whāriki. He whāriki mātauranga mō ngā mokopuna o Aotearoa: Early Childhood Curriculum*. Wellington: Learning Media. Retrieved from http://www.educate.ece.

govt.nz/~/media/Educate/Files/Reference%20Downloads/whariki.pdf.

New Zealand Parliament. (1862). Further Report on Native Schools in the Province of Auckland, Appendix to the Journals of the House of Representatives of New Zealand (Vol. July–Sept). Wellington: New Zealand Parliament. Retrieved from http://books.google.co.nz/books?id=dwFQAAAAYAAJ&pg=RA4-PA35&lpg=RA4PA35&dq=%22would+to+a+native+seem+cruel+and+excessive%22&source=bl&ots=2bgnQvl82o&sig=14DaFoKr_kzHvhfwjbAS7LsMeNM&hl=en&ei=6864TeumKo6IvgPP2pGiAw&sa=X&oi=book_result&ct=result&resnum=2&sqi=2&ved=0CBoQ6AEwAQ#v=onepage&q=%.

Orange, C. (1987). *The Treaty of Waitangi*. Wellington: Allen and Unwin/Port Nicholson Press.

Policy Strategy and Research Group Department of Corrections. (2007). Over-representation of Māori in the criminal justice system. An exploratory report. Wellington, NZ: Department of Corrections. Retrieved from: http://www.corrections.govt.nz/__data/assets/pdf_file/0004/285286/Over-representation-of-Maori-in-the-criminal-justice-system.pdf.

Ritchie, J. (1978). *Chance to be Equal*. Queen Charlotte Sound: Cape Catley.

Ritchie, J. (2002). *"It's Becoming Part of Their Knowing": A Study of Bicultural Development in an Early Childhood Teacher Education Setting in Aotearoa/New Zealand*. Ph.D. thesis, University of Waikato, Hamilton.

Rose, N., & Novas, C. (2005). Biological citizenship. In A. Ong & S. J. Collier (Eds), *Global Assemblages: Technologies, Politics, and Ethics as Anthropological Problems* (pp. 439–463). Malden, MA: Blackwell.

Salmond, Anne. (1991). *Two Worlds: First Meetings between Māori and Europeans, 1642–1772*. Auckland: Viking.

Shallcrass, J. (1978). Introduction. In J. Ritchie (Ed.), *Chance to be Equal* (pp. xv–xvii). Whatamongo Bay, Queen Charlotte Sound: Cape Cately.

Simon, J. (1989). Aspirations and ideology: biculturalism and multiculturalism in New Zealand Education. *Sites, 18*, 23–34.

Simon, J. (1996). Good intentions, but... In R. Steele (Ed.), *Whakamana Tangata* (pp. 38–42). Wellington: Quest Rapuara.

Skerrett, M. (2007). Kia Tū Heipū: languages frame, focus and colour our worlds. *Childrenz Issues, 11*(1), 6–14.

Smith, G. H. (1990). Taha Maori: Pakeha Capture. In J. Codd, R. Harker, & R. Nash (Eds), *Political Issues in New Zealand Education* (2nd ed., pp. 183–197). Palmerston North: Dunmore.

Smith, L. (1991). *Education Reform Bill: Second Reading*. New Zealand Parliamentary Debate, New Zealand Hansard. Retrieved from: http://www.vdig.net/hansard/archive.jsp?y=1991&m=12&d=10&o=153&p=168.

Waitangi T. (1986). Report of the Waitangi Tribunal on the Te Reo Maori Claim (WAI 11). Wellington: GP Publications: Waitangi Tribunal. Retrieved from http://www.waitangi-tribunal.govt.nz/reports/default.asp?type=wai&keywords=11.

Walker, R. (1985). Cultural domination of Taha Maori: the potential for radical transformation. In J. Codd, R. Harker, & R. Nash (Eds), *Political Issues in New Zealand Education*. Palmerston North: Dunmore.

Walker, R. (2004). *Ka Whawhai Tonu Matou. Struggle without End* (revised ed.). Auckland: Penguin.

5
Post-*Te Whāriki* Early Childhood Care and Education Policy and Practice in "Whitestream" Early Childhood Care and Education in Aotearoa[1]

Jenny Ritchie

Abstract: *This chapter provides a brief context for the early childhood curriculum* Te Whāriki. He whāriki mātauranga mō ngā mokopuna o Aotearoa, *which set in place the expectation of a radically different notion of curriculum, in its non-prescriptive philosophical, socio-cultural, holistic, and bicultural nature. Not the least of these challenges was the delivery of a curriculum inclusive of the Māori culture and language by a predominately non-Māori teacher workforce. The promulgation of* Te Whāriki *provoked the need for articulation of applied pedagogies in support of its bicultural expectations. A range of Ministry of Education documents that were subsequently promulgated, aimed at enhancing the delivery of the bicultural curriculum are overviewed. Acknowledgment is made that the aspirations of* Te Whāriki *are still in the process of becoming.*

Ritchie J., and M. Skerrett. *Early Childhood Education in Aotearoa New Zealand: History, Pedagogy, and Liberation.*
New York: Palgrave Macmillan, 2014.
DOI: 10.1057/9781137375797.0009.

> Te manu ka kai i te miro, nōna te ngāhere; te manu ka kai i te mātauranga, nōna te ao.
>
> The bird that feeds on miro berries reigns in the forest; the bird that feeds on knowledge has access to the world. (Mead & Mead, 2010, p. 74)

Background

Despite the initially honorable intentions of the British Crown as expressed in the 1840 *Tiriti o Waitangi*/Treaty of Waitangi, which allowed for British settlement of Aotearoa, entrenched attitudes of white supremacy led inevitably to a legacy of colonization. Through this process Māori were divested of their lands and self-determination, and their traditional values, knowledges, and language threatened to the point of extinction, despite *Te Tiriti*/The Treaty's explicitly expressed intent of protection of these. The colonial education system, which Mere Skerrett (in this volume) has termed "whitestream" education, was dismissive of traditional Māori childrearing practices.

Māori traditionally had great respect for children, who were encouraged and supported by the wider collective in a shared parenting model. They were treated with great indulgence and seldom punished. The colonial system reflected its roots in Great Britain, where punishment was routine. This unfortunately resulted in generations of Māori students being beaten for speaking their own language, with the end result that many stopped speaking Māori with their children, in order to protect them. Schooling became associated with punishment, pain, and lack of validation of one's identity. Education for Māori students reflected the dominant *Pākehā* (of European ancestry) society, with Māori knowledges consciously and unconsciously denigrated, and was intended to prepare Māori for working-class employment. The outcome of these policies is not surprising. Deficit discourses became deeply embedded within New Zealand society and "whitestream" education. Māori have continuously been over-represented amongst the students who leave school with few or no qualifications, as well as consistently featuring negatively within the justice, health, and economic statistics.

As has been outlined in the previous chapter, from the late 1800s onward, a range of grass-roots ECCE organizations came into being, each born out of a response to particular community circumstances, as well as reflecting to varying degrees the international influences of Froebel, Montessori, and Deweyan philosophies. These services remained outside of the compulsory education sector. This lack of government involvement in the sector had the effect of allowing for freedom and responsiveness to the community. However, this positioning also meant that ECCE services were under-funded and under-resourced.

1990 was the year when New Zealand commemorated the bicentenary of the signing of The Treaty of Waitangi. A greater awareness of the treaty was generated in the *Pākehā* community at this time (Māori communities had always maintained a commitment to *Te Tiriti o Waitangi*, consistently calling for the Crown (government) to adhere to its obligations under the Treaty). Responsiveness was particularly evident in the ECCE sector to Māori demand for the promises of the 1840 *Tiriti*/Treaty to be acknowledged. This sensitivity informed the development of *Te Whāriki*, which modeled a process of partnership (between Crown representatives and Māori) amongst the writers. Helen May and Margaret Carr of the University of Waikato led the writing and consultative process along with Tamati and Tilly Reedy, who had been nominated by the National Te Kōhanga Reo Trust to write a separate Māori early childhood curriculum to form an integral part of the document. The Māori philosophical framework that the Reedys provided also informed the entire curriculum document, resulting in "a national curriculum whose conceptual framework is based on the cultural and political beliefs of the minority Indigenous people" (Te One, 2003, p. 19). It is anomalous that this progressive, innovative, bicultural curriculum was produced during an era of neo-iberal/neoconservative government, which is backgrounded in the following section.

Neoliberal discursive era

New Zealand during the 1980s and 1990s experienced an extreme conversion to neoliberal doctrine, resulting in deregulation, devolution, corporatization, and privatization of services such as education that had previously been held as the domain of the state (Farquhar, 2008), in what has been described as "the most ambitious attempt at constructing the free market as a social institution to be introduced anywhere this century" (Gray, 1998, p. 39, as cited in Farquhar, 2008, p. 119). After many years of priding itself on being a "welfare state" that cared for all its citizens, "New Zealand moved almost overnight to a user pays, market driven economic system," welfare systems were pruned and national assets privatized (Carpenter, 2009, p. 3). New Zealand early childhood services have been increasingly privatized in line with the international Organisation for Economic Co-operation and Development (OECD) policy, which aims to "limit public expenditure and to allow greater choice and control by parents" (Farquhar, 2008, p. 125). The traditionally left-wing Labour government (1984–1990) whilst captured by neoliberalist economics, tried to maintain a commitment to social justice and the traditional Labour government ethic of egalitarianism in its social policy-making. Owing to Māori activism within the party, it also had significant commitments to The Treaty of Waitangi. The curriculum reforms initiated under this government included the *Before Five* (Lange, 1988) policy document, and led to the development of *Te Whāriki*, both of which reflected this commitment.

The right-wing National Party formed the next government (1990–1999), and immediately delivered policy changes reflecting a more extreme neoliberal/neoconservative doctrine, rendering it somewhat bizarre that *Te Whāriki* was produced during this decade. Understanding this seeming anomaly requires unpacking the complexities of the assemblage of the early childhood sector, as outlined in the previous chapter, as a "flax-roots" loose collective of different organizations, all deeply committed to offering services for children and families in particular contexts. From a Deleuze-Guattarian perspective, the ECCE sector in Aotearoa, and *Te Whāriki*, can be seen as assemblages that are "passional, they are compositions of desire" (Deleuze & Guattari, 2004, p. 440), and that were collectively strong enough to resist the striations being imposed by neoliberal policies. It has also been suggested that the National Government Minister of Education may have been uninterested in closely monitoring the development of a curriculum for a non-compulsory education sector that was largely the domain of women and young children (Mutch & Trim, 2013).

Neoliberalism has been described as a "heightening and renewal of modernity's now dominant metanarrative" of individuals as "rational utility maximisers" (Peters, 2001, p. 119). Recent neoliberal metanarratives "reframe *all* human transactions as being primarily economic in nature" (Cope & I'Anson, 2003, p. 220). Forces/forcers of international globalization such as the International Monetary Fund and the World Bank have promulgated "a Western-centered architecture for global capitalism" (Robertson & Dale, 2009, p. 32), resulting in "the triumph of market fundamentalism" infiltrating what were previously social services, and education being remodeled as a marketable commodity (Saltman, 2009, p. 56). This discursive shift is seen in the education curriculum documents that promote the "ability to earn money, flexibility, [and] competitiveness" as opposed to previously celebrated values for maintaining the social fabric such as "solidarity, fairness, and compassion" (McCarthy, Pitton, Kim, & Monje, 2009, pp. 40–41).

The workings of neoliberalism create a sense of positioning for educational (and other) services that is deliberately (and artificially) detached from the direct engagement of government, a form of governmentality that allows the governmental officers to maintain a sense of independence from any calamities that ensue, since "Risk management is forced back onto individuals and satisfied through the market" (Peters, 2001, p. 111). The perils of this approach was supremely evident in the tragedy of the recent Fukushima disaster in Japan (Stiglitz, 2010). Meanwhile, corporate, middle-class bureaucratic capture promotes individualism in the forms of consumer autonomy, privatization, user-pays, and individual enterprise (Peters, 2001), which are in contrast to Indigenous values of collectivism. Ironically the individual also becomes relatively powerless to oppose these forces, as "our contemporary capitalist society adjusts to changes, and works to refold rogue elements of the socius back into the ceaseless play of the commodity" (Roffe, 2007, p. 48). As neoliberal subjects are required to become "entrepreneurs of themselves" (Foucault, 1979, as cited in McCarthy et al., 2009, p. 40), individual "freedom" is positioned "as being more important than welfare liberalism's privileging of equality" (Farquhar, 2008, p. 17).

The ECCE sector in Aotearoa had been dramatically affected by neoliberal policies, seen particularly in the shift toward privatization. In 2000, 26 percent of early childhood centers were privately owned profit-making businesses, whilst a decade later, in 2010, 40 percent of our early childhood provision operated as "for-profit" businesses (ECE Taskforce Secretariat, 2010, p. 5). This situation has rendered children, families, and teachers vulnerable to "market failure" (Farquhar, 2008, p. 126). New Zealand has therefore become "a culture where the market is regarded as the ethic guiding all human action, [and] the subject's identity is constructed in and by the market" (McCarthy et al., 2009, p. 40). Recent research has identified increasing discrepancies in the provision of ECCE, with many low-income, Māori, and Pacific Islands families struggling to access services (Ritchie & Johnson, 2011). The reterritorializing by this intensifying neoliberal metanarrative seems devoid of an ethic of care, or of the egalitarianism that was once a professed characteristic of New Zealand society, albeit with the ongoing under-belly of racism and colonization. Corporate interests prevail, a hegemonic faith in the mythological market side-lining Māori interests, despite the ostensible role of the Māori Party within a National-led coalition government.

Te Whāriki as a kaupapa Māori vision

Not only was *Te Whāriki* the first ECCE curriculum for New Zealand, it was also the first "bicultural" and bilingual education curriculum for the country. The introduction of the document contains the commitment that "In early childhood settings, all children should be given the opportunity to develop knowledge and an understanding of the cultural heritages of both partners to Te Tiriti o Waitangi" (New Zealand Ministry of Education, 1996b, p. 9). It contains a section written in the Māori language intended for Māori-medium settings (pp. 31–39), as well as the integration of expectations pertaining to inclusion of Māori language and content interspersed throughout the document. An example from the Māori section of *Te Whāriki* reads that: "Mā te whai mana o te mokopuna ka taea e ia te tū kaha i runga i tōna mana Māori motuhake me tōna tino rangatiratanga" (New Zealand Ministry of Education, 1996b, p. 32) ["Through the pursuit of pride, prestige, and authority the child will be able to stand strongly in her/his sense of Māori independence and self-determination"—author's translation]. Te Whāriki contains currents strongly reflective of social justice, such as in this example from the Strand Belonging: "Strategies for managing behaviour are used not only to prevent unacceptable behaviour but also to develop ideas of fairness and justice and to introduce new social skills" (New Zealand Ministry of Education, 1996b, p. 63). The curriculum was ground-breaking not only for Aotearoa, but also internationally, in the prominence given to recognition of Indigeneity within regular state educational provision, the dominance of Western early childhood discourses being "rightfully counterbalanced" by Māori worldviews (Fleer, 2013, p. 221).

The Indigenization of the curriculum can be seen in the structure of the document, which foregrounds a separate Māori text, "Part B," intended for Māori immersion services such as Kōhanga Reo (pp. 31–38). The Māori text whilst described in the Table of Contents as "an integral part of the document" (p. 4) is actually a curriculum within a curriculum. The remainder of the document is intended for services that are not Māori immersion, that is, the vast majority of services in Aotearoa, in which the main medium of education is English. The principles, strands goals, and learning outcomes detailed in "Part C" of the document reflect an integration of te ao Māori aspirations. *Te Whāriki* has four over-arching principles: Empowerment/Whakamana; Holistic Development/Kotahitanga; Family and Community/Whānau Tangata; and Relationships/Ngā Hononga. Intervoven with these principles are the five strands of the curriculum: Well-Being/Mana Atua; Belonging/Mana Whenua; Contribution/Mana Tangata; Contribution/Mana Reo; and Exploration/Mana Aotūroa. By way of example of this integration, the explanation of the principle of Whānau Tangata/Families and Communities states that:

> New Zealand is the home of Māori language and culture: curriculum in early childhood settings should promote te reo and ngā tikanga Māori [Māori language and cultural beliefs and practices], making them visible and affirming their value for children from all cultural backgrounds. Adults working with children should demonstrate an understanding of the different iwi [tribes] and the meaning of whānau [extended families] and wh[a]naungatanga [relationships]. They should also respect the aspirations of parents and families for their children. (New Zealand Ministry of Education, 1996b, p. 42)

The kaupapa Māori (Māori philosophical) framework arguably provides an important structural and philosophical coherence to the document, given its depth and complexity. *Te Whāriki* is recognized for its "theoretical plurality" (Fleer, 2013, p. 217) in simultaneously drawing upon a wide range of theorists and paradigms, including socio-cultural, constructivist, cognitivist, and developmentalist views (Fleer, 2013; Ministry of Education, 1993).

Concerns have long been expressed about the capacity of the early childhood education profession to deliver on the expectations of *Te Whāriki*, not just in regard to the lack of (bi)cultural competency, but because of the complexity of delivering a curriculum that requires a sophisticated range of dispositions on the part of educators (Cullen, 2003; May, 2009). One of the writers of *Te Whāriki*, Helen May, considered that "the holistic and bicultural approach to curriculum of Te Whāriki, inclusive of children from birth, was a challenge to staff who were more familiar with the traditional focus on play areas and activities for children in mainstream centres" (May, 2001, p. 248). Whilst in previous writing I have taken the optimistic view that Te Whāriki is a document of promise that can serve as a lever for change toward counter-colonial pedagogies (Ritchie, 2003a, 2005, 2013), early childhood educators have acknowledged ongoing challenges in the realization of its potential as a "bicultural" document (Ritchie, 2003b; Ritchie & Rau, 2006).

In addition to and in accordance with the affirmation of the status of Māori as *tangata whenua* (people of the land—Indigenous peoples), *Te Whāriki* is strongly socio-cultural, rather than solely developmentalist. It requires educators to acknowledge and represent the values and belief systems of not only Māori and Pākehā (those with European ancestry) but of *all* children and their families attending that ECCE center, recognizing their identities and learning as being sourced in their nature as *cultural* beings (Rogoff, 2003). *Te Whāriki* goes beyond a merely "child-centered" approach, drawing upon *te ao* Māori (Māori worldview) influences as seen in the foundational principles of Whakamana/Empowerment and Ngā Hononga/Relationships to define these pedagogically significant relationships as inclusive of *whānau/* parents. Another example of *te ao* Maori conceptualizations having reconfigured dominant Western discoures can be seen in the key strand of Mana Atua/Well-being, which adopts a holistic, integrative focus on emotional and spiritual as well as physical well-being. The curriculum highlights the roles of dispositions and working theories in children's learning (p. 44), which are to be strengthened through dialogical engagement within learning communities. Inherent, although not explicit, within Te Whāriki, is an understanding of the importance of narrative, and that these narratives can be the result of collaborative processes of co-constructed meaning-making (Jordan, 2009) and are also a means of intergenerational knowledge transmission (Lee, 2005). Learning in this view is a process of storying, reified through careful and respectful listening and documentation.

Early childhood educators were widely consulted in the development of *Te Whāriki*, and were generally supportive, yet concern was expressed about the preparedness of a sector, which was at that time dominated by unqualified teachers, to deliver such a complex and challenging curriculum (Cullen, 2003; May, 2001). Furthermore, the sector was dominated by *Pākehā* (of European ancestry) educators, the vast majority of whom had only a superficial knowledge of Māori language and culture. A sociocultural critique of the delivery of programs over the past two decades could well ask a range questions as to: whose cultures and languages are being represented?; in what ways and to what degree of authenticity are these represented?; and how deeply are educators engaging with the specificities of individual children and families regarding their histories, values, and passions? From a Deleuzian perspective, *Te Whāriki* might be considered to be a "plan(e)" that "can only be inferred from the forms it develops and the subjects it forms" (Deleuze & Guattari, 2004, p. 293). In the remainder of this chapter I provide an overview of key Ministry of Education documents that form part of the ever-shifting assemblage of *Te Whāriki*, reflecting "relations of movement and rest, speed and slowness between unformed elements" (Deleuze & Guattari, 2004, p. 293).

Ministry of Education guidance

The New Zealand Ministry of Education, aware of the challenges facing the then predominately unqualified early childhood sector in delivering *Te Whāriki*, funded a range of in-service professional learning opportunities, and also rolled out a series of documents in support of curriculum enactment. Directly after the promulgation of *Te Whāriki*, the Ministry produced a *"Revised Statement of Desirable Objectives and Practices (DOPs) for Chartered Early Childhood Services in New Zealand"* (New Zealand Ministry of Education, 1996a), which brought these objectives and practices into alignment with the recently released new curriculum *Te Whāriki*. DOPs number 10 states that "Management and educators should implement policies, objectives and practices which:

(a) reflect the service's philosophy, quality curriculum, current theories of learning and development, the requirements of the DOPs and legislation;
(b) acknowledge parents/guardians and whānau [families'] needs and aspirations for their child;
(c) reflect the unique place of Māori as tangata whenua [Indigenous people of New Zealand] and the principle of partnership inherent in Te Tiriti o Waitangi;

(d) are inclusive, equitable and culturally appropriate;
(e) are regularly evaluated and modified by an on-going, recorded process of internal review" (New Zealand Ministry of Education, 1996a, p. 2).

The positioning of recognition of both Māori as *tangata whenua* and of *Te Tiriti o Waitangi* at tenth of a list of 12 items is telling. Interestingly *Te Whāriki* was not referred to in the entire document, although the *Te Whāriki* aspiration statement is positioned as a "Guiding Principle" of the Revised DOPs and content from the principles and strands of *Te Whāriki* is interwoven throughout.

Recognition that implementing *Te Whāriki* was perceived as daunting by many within the largely unqualified early childhood sector led the Ministry of Education to provide a supporting document to the Revised DOPs, which was called "*Quality in Action. Te Mahi Whai hua*" (New Zealand Ministry of Education, 1998). It contained an integrated series of "Bicultural Approaches" throughout its series of explanations of "desirable" practices. Under DOP5(a), where educators should "plan, implement and evaluate curriculum for children in which their helath is promoted and emotional well-being nurtured, and they are kept safe from harm" (New Zealand Ministry of Education, 1998, p. 41), the document begins the relevant section of "Bicultural Approaches" with the statement recognizing the integral importance of "taha wairua (spiritual wellbeing)" to not only tamariki Māori (Māori children) but also "to the well-being of all children in their service" (p. 42). In scoping the writers and writing process for this document, the Ministry had clearly followed a *Tiriti o Waitangi* based model, as was instigated by Helen May and Margaret Carr in the production of Te Whāriki, in foregrounding *te ao* Māori (Māori worldview) within this supporting document.

In recognition that strengthening the "quality" (and "bicultural") provision was an ongoing and challenging requirement, and in response to neoconservative ideologies of accountability and "quality assurance" in relation to public spending, the Ministry in 1999 released a document designed to enhance "quality" provision in the sector, "*The quality journey. He haerenga whai hua*" (New Zealand Ministry of Education, 1999). In its introductory pages, the document included "the principle of partnership inherent in Te Tiriti o Waitangi" as one "touchstone of quality improvement" and asked services to reflect on how well they were supporting Māori children and communicating with their *whānau* (families), and upon the extent to which staff incorporated Māori language and culture and beliefs within their service (p. 6). This document was not widely picked up within the sector, possibly because of an intuited distrust of being captured by the managerialist emphasis of the neoconservative/neoliberal National government of the day, which infused the document with managerialist languaging such as "Developing a Quality Improvement System" (p. 8). As a response to the lack of uptake of *"The Quality Journey,"* another document outlining processes for center review was subsequently produced, which continued the *Te Whāriki* metaphor of weaving the curriculum, *"Ngā Arohaehae Whai Hua. Self-review guidelines for ECE"* (New Zealand Ministry of Education, 2006).

The 2002 strategic plan for the sector, instigated and promoted by the incoming Labour-led government, *"Pathways to the Future: Ngā Huarahi Arataki"* (New Zealand Ministry of Education, 2002) contained reinforcement of the need for educators to work "in partnership" with families, and in particular, Māori and Pacific Island families to support their children's education. This focus can be interpreted as compensatory (remedying impacts of colonization) and/or as reflecting a monetarist neoliberal anxiety about future economic impacts of a large Māori and Pacific unskilled workforce (Nuttall, 2005). The strategic plan also outlined a staged program to reach the goal of requiring all ECCE teachers to become qualified by the year 2012. Sadly, the change of government in 2008 meant that this expectation was reduced to a 50 percent minimum. Also under the goal of "improving the quality of ECE services" was the "vision for mainstream services [to be] more responsive to Māori [by] 2012," with an example given that:

> Māori children attending mainstream ECE services have their learning and development extended by teachers who are competent in Te Reo [the Māori language], at least being able to pronounce Māori names correctly. These teachers understand and acknowledge Te Tiriti o Waitangi and Māori cultural values. They work in partnership with local hapū [subtribes], iwi [tribes] and the Māori community generally to deliver effectively to Māori children in their service. (New Zealand Ministry of Education, 2002, p. 14)

This extremely limited aspiration of "at least" being able to pronounce Māori children's names correctly in ten years' time sits awkwardly at odds with the broader, deeper cultural competencies required by non-Māori teachers in order to enact the rest of the espoused vision.

Further documents produced by the Ministry for the early childhood sector, and ostensibly reinforcing the "bicultural" stance of *Te Whāriki*, include a series of booklets of examples of assessment, which follow a narrative paradigm, entitled *Kei Tua o te Pae. Assessment for learning: Early Childhood Exemplars* (New Zealand Ministry of Education, 2004, 2007, 2009). Booklet Three of the 20 series of 20 booklets focuses on *"Bicultural Assessment"* (Ministry of Education, 2004). The other 19 booklets generally lack examples of bicultural practice whereby te ao Māori (Māori worldview) perspectives are integrated into the "learning stories." For example, Booklet 12, focused on the strand of Well-Being/Mana Atua contains no learning story reflecting the central importance in te ao Māori (Māori worldview) of spiritual well-being (in fact there is no mention at all of spiritual well-being) despite "spiritual dimensions" being recognized as significant to Māori and Pacific Islands peoples in the Well-being Strand of *Te Whāriki* (New Zealand Ministry of Education, 1996b, p. 46). In response to concerns raised by Māori educators, a further assessment document was produced. *"Te Whatu Pōkeka"* (New Zealand Ministry of Education, 2009) has a particular focus on the assessment of Māori children. The latter document received only minimal financial support from the Ministry of Education for professional learning to upskill teachers in comparison to the hefty funding provided for *Kei Tua o te Pae*.

In 2011 the Ministry of Education and the New Zealand Teachers Council, the professional body that oversees both teaching qualification provision and individual teacher registration, released a jointly produced document, *Tātaiako: Cultural Competencies for Teachers of Māori Learners* (New Zealand Ministry of Education & New Zealand Teachers Council, 2011). Since all teachers in Aotearoa will inevitably teach Māori learners, it seems obvious that the document would have been better titled *"Kaupapa Māori Competencies for Teachers."* Choosing to entitle the document as being for "teachers of Māori learners" allows "whitestream"-thinking teachers to dismiss the document as being irrelevant to them. *Tātaiako* was produced to align with *Ka Hikitia Managing for Success. Māori Education Strategy 2008–2012* (New Zealand Ministry of Education, 2008), stressing the importance of "identity, language and culture—teachers knowing where their students come from, and building on what students bring with them; and on productive partnerships among teachers, Māori learners, whānau [families], and iwi [tribes]" (New Zealand Ministry of Education & New Zealand Teachers Council, 2011, p. 4). The competencies for teachers in Aotearoa outlined in *Tātaiako* are defined as follows:

- *Wānanga*: Participating with learners and communities in robust dialogue for the benefit of Māori learners' achievement.
- *Whanaungatanga*: Actively engaging in respectful working relationships with Māori learners, parents and whānau [families], hapū [sub-tribes], iwi [tribes], and the Māori community.
- *Manaakitanga*: Showing integrity, sincerity, and respect toward Māori beliefs, language, and culture.
- *Tangata Whenuatanga*: Affirming Māori learners as Māori. Providing contexts for learning where the language, identity, and culture of Māori learners and their whānau is affirmed.
- *Ako*: Taking responsibility for their own learning and that of Māori learners. (New Zealand Ministry of Education & New Zealand Teachers Council, 2011, p. 4)

These competencies contain dispositions of humility, positioning teachers as learners alongside their students, and requiring pro-activity on the part of teachers from the dominant, "whitestream" culture to genuinely engage in relationship-building with Māori children, families, and communities. Furthermore, these competencies require a certain depth of experience and understanding in order for teachers to recognize and affirm Māori knowledges. In the following section, recent reporting by the government's review agency demonstrates that these dispositions and knowledges are currently lacking in the ECCE workforce.

Reviewing implementation

The Education Review Office (ERO) is the New Zealand government agency charged with reviewing the delivery of education programs by ECCE centers and schools. In addition to regularly visiting and reporting on individual centers and schools, the ERO produces an ongoing series of wider national reports. Several recent reports have highlighted practices in relation to *tamariki* Māori (Māori children) in ECCE services (Education Review Office, 2008, 2010a, 2010b, 2012). A 2008 pilot study of 17 services reported that in only "just over half the services Māori children had opportunities to develop as confident and competent learners through programs that included aspects of te reo and tikanga Māori" (Māori language and cultural practices) (Education Review Office, 2008, p. 1). In this and the subsequent larger study of 576 centers, assimilatory pedagogies were prevalent in that many teachers and managers said that they "treated all children the same" (Education Review Office, 2008, 2010a) and that their aspirations for Māori children were the same as for other children, indicating that they had not bothered to find out what Māori parents/*whānau* aspirations for their children might be. Rhetoric was not transferred into practice, since although most services included reference to Māori perspectives in documentation such as their philosophy statement and policies, these were not applied within daily practice. In addition, many services lacked adequate self-review processes to evaluate the effectiveness of their provision for Māori children (Education Review Office, 2008, 2010a).

Also of concern is that, "Although many services implemented what they considered to be a bicultural curriculum, the quality and relevance of this was variable. Managers and educators did not yet fully recognize the importance of acknowledging Māori children's cultural identity and heritage" (Education Review Office, 2010a, p. 2). That this was the scenario a decade and a half after *Te Whāriki* had explicitly stated the *Tiriti o Waitangi* commitments of the ECCE sector is worrying indeed and calls into question the adequacy of infrastructural and resourcing supports for early childhood teachers. What are the alternate currents, the "desiring machines" that serve to reinforce the power relations that reterritorialize/invisibilize *te ao* Māori (Māori worldview) priorities, despite the reiteration of these within mandated documents?

Attaining and maintaining momentum

Providers of initial teacher education are potential sites of transformation, in the possibilities that they afford their students to understand the importance of their role as cultural workers (Freire, 2005) in service of social and cultural justice praxis (Freire, 1972). Integral to this process is to generate within their graduates an understanding of the history of colonization in this country, which has necessitated the current situation of an imperative for pedagogical redress (Ritchie, 2002), most critically and recently expressed in the need to shift from a "deficit" to a capability orientation (New Zealand Ministry of Education, 2013). Rather than treating all children "the same" (Education Review Office, 2008; Simon, 1996), that is, producing pedagogy dominated by a middle-class *Pākehā* (of European ancestry) perspective, graduates need to be prepared to act as agents of transformation within ECCE centers where management and staff are comfortable with monocultural Western approaches and lack the commitment and knowledge required to implement the kaupapa Māori (Māori philosophy) expectations contained within *Te Whāriki* and in other Ministry of Education documents. Ongoing support and professional learning for both beginning teachers and their mentors is crucial to obtaining and maintaining these professional commitments, particularly in teaching settings that are unsupportive of these philosophies (Aitken, Piggot-Irvine, Bruce Ferguson, McGrath, & Ritchie, 2008; Piggot-Irvine, Aitken, Ritchie, Bruce Ferguson, & McGrath, 2009). The New Zealand Teachers Council has recently been reviewed, and it will be interesting to see if the outcome of the review produces enhancements of these dual functions with regard to strengthening kaupapa Māori provision within "whitestream" education settings.

This chapter has provided an overview of documents produced by the Ministry of Education subsequent to *Te Whāriki*, and has argued that despite dedicated sections focused on commitments pertaining to *Te Tiriti o Waitangi*, selective uptake of the documents' contents has meant that *te ao* Māori conceptualizations remain marginalized in many centers. The next chapter draws upon recent research to illustrate some ways in which early childhood educators are demonstrating commitment to aspirations of *Te Tiriti o Waitangi* and *Te Whāriki*, in relation to pedagogies resonant with *te ao* Māori ways of being, knowing, and doing.

> *E kore au e ngaro he kākano i ruia mai i Rangiatea*
>
> *This whakatauki refers to the original seed from Rangiatea, the spiritual homeland for Māori, stating that this seed will not be lost. It thus asserts both continuity and resilience, and implies that for Māori, their language and culture are the sustenance of this resilience* (Grace & Grace, 2003, p. 29).

Note

1. An earlier version of this chapter appeared in a special edition of *Pacific-Asia Education* entitled "Past, present and future: Conceptualisations of Early Childhood Education in the Pacific-Asian region" (vol. 24, issue 2, 2012).

My chapter in that edition was entitled *An overview of early childhood care and education provision in "mainstream" settings, in relation to kaupapa Māori curriculum and policy expectations*. We thank the editors of this journal for granting us permission to base this chapter on the article.

References

Aitken, H., Piggot-Irvine, E., Bruce Ferguson, P., McGrath, F., & Ritchie, J. (2008). *Learning to Teach: Success Case Studies of Teacher Induction in Aotearoa New Zealand*. Wellington: New Zealand Teachers Council.

Carpenter, V. (2009). *Education, Teachers and the Children of the Poor*. Keynote address at the Researching Professionals Symposium, University of Otago College of Education, Dunedin, July 15.

Cope, P., & I'Anson, J. (2003). Forms of exchange: education, economics and the neglect of social contingency. *British Journal of Educational Studies, 51*(3), 219–232.

Cullen, J. (2003). The challenge of Te Whāriki: catalyst for change? In J. Nuttall (Ed.), *Weaving Te Whāriki. Aotearoa New Zealand's Early Childhood Curriculum Document in Theory and Practice* (pp. 269–296). Wellington: New Zealand Council for Educational Research.

Deleuze, G., & Guattari, F. (2004). *A Thousand Plateaus: Capitalism and Schizophrenia* (B. Massumi, Trans.). London and New York: Continuum.

ECE Taskforce Secretariat. (2010). *Overview of the New Zealand Early Childhood Education (ECE) System: Introductory Briefing*. Wellington: New Zealand Ministry of Education. Retrieved from http://www.taskforce.ece.govt.nz/wp-content/uploads/2010/11/1-Overview-of-the-NZ-Early-Childhood-Education-System.pdf.

Education Review Office. (2008). *Māori Children in Early Childhood: Pilot Study*. Wellington: Education Review Office.

Education Review Office. (2010a). *Success for Māori Children in Early Childhood Services*. Wellington: Education Review Office.

Education Review Office. (2010b). *Success for Māori Children in Early Childhood Services: Good Practice*. Wellington: Education Review Office.

Education Review Office. (2012). *Partnership with whānau Māori in Early Childhood Services*. Wellington: Education Review Office.

Farquhar, S. (2008). *Narrative Identity, Ricoeur and Early Childhood Education.* Doctor of Philosophy Thesis. The University of Auckland, Auckland.

Fleer, M. (2003). The many voices of Te Whāriki: Kaupapa Māori, socio-cultural, developmental, constructivist, and ...? Australians listen carefully. In J. Nuttall (Ed.), *Weaving Te Whāriki: Aotearoa New Zealand's Early Childhood Curriculum Document in Theory and Practice.* Wellington: NZCER.

Fleer, M. (2013). Theoretical plurality in curriculum design: the many voices of Te Whāriki and the early years learning framework. In J. Nuttall (Ed.), *Weaving Te Whāriki* (2nd ed., pp. 217–238). Wellington: NZCER Press.

Freire, P. (1972). *Pedagogy of the Oppressed.* London: Penguin.

Freire, P. (2005). *Teachers as Cultural Workers: Letters to Those Who Dare Teach.* Boulder, Colorado: Westview Press.

Jenkins, K., & Harte, H. M. (2011). *Traditional Maori Parenting: An Historical Review of Literature of Traditional Maori Child Rearing Practices in Pre-European Times.* Auckland: Te Kahui Mana Ririki. Retrieved from http://www.whakawhetu.co.nz/assets/files/TraditionalMaoriParenting.pdf.

Jordan, B. (2009). Scaffolding learning and co-constructing understandings. In A. Anning, J. Cullen, & M. Fleer (Eds), *Early Childhood Education: Society and Culture* (pp. 39–52). Los Angeles: Sage.

Lange, D. (1988). *Before Five: Early Childhood Care and Education in New Zealand.* Wellington: Department of Education.

Lee, J. (2005). *Māori Cultural Regeneration: Pūrākau as Pedagogy. Paper Presented as Part of a Symposium "Indigenous (Māori) Pedagogies:Towards Community and Cultural Regeneration."* Paper presented at the Centre for Research in Lifelong Learning International Conference, Stirling, Scotland. Retrieved from www.kaupapamaori.com/assets//crll_final.pdf.

May, H. (1997). *The Discovery of Early Childhood.* Auckland: Bridget Williams Books, Auckland University Press.

May, H. (2001). *Politics in the Playground: The World of Early Childhood in Postwar New Zealand.* Wellington: Bridget Williams Books and New Zealand Council for Educational Research.

May, H. (2009). *Politics in the Playground: The World of Early Childhood in New Zealand* (2nd ed.). Dunedin: Otago University Press.

McCarthy, C., Pitton, V., Kim, S., & Monje, D. (2009). Movement and stasis in the neoliberal reorientation of schools. In M. Apple, W. W. Au & L. A. Gandin (Eds), *The Routledge International Handbook of Critical Education* (pp. 36–50). New York: Routledge.

Ministry of Education. (1993). *Te Whāriki, Draft Guidelines for Developmentally Appropriate Programmes in Early Childhood*. Wellington: Learning Media.

Ministry of Health. (2006). Decades of Disparity III: Ethnic and Socioeconomic Inequalities in Mortality, New Zealand 1988–1999. *Public Health Intelligence Occasional Bulletin Number 31*. Wellington: Ministry of Health and University of Otago. Retrieved from http://www.moh.govt.nz/notebook/nbbooks.nsf/0/37a7abb191191fb9cc256d da00064211/$FILE/EthnicMortalityTrends.pdf.

Mutch, C., & Trim, B. (2013). Improvement, accountability and sustainability. In J. Nuttall (Ed.), *Weaving Te Whāriki: Aotearoa New Zealand's Curriculum Document in Theory and Practice* (2nd ed., pp. 71–91). Wellington: NZCER Press.

New Zealand Ministry of Education. (1996a). Revised Statement of Desirable Objectives and Practices (DOPs) for Chartered Early Childhood Services in New Zealand. *Supplement to the Education Gazette*. Wellington: Ministry of Education.

New Zealand Ministry of Education. (1996b). *Te Whāriki. He whāriki mātauranga mō ngā mokopuna o Aotearoa: Early Childhood Curriculum*. Wellington: Learning Media. Retrieved from http://www.educate.ece. govt.nz/~/media/Educate/Files/Reference%20Downloads/whariki.pdf.

New Zealand Ministry of Education. (1998). *Quality in Action: Te Mahi Whai Hua*. Wellington: Learning Media.

New Zealand Ministry of Education. (1999). *The Quality Journey: He haerenga whai hua*. Wellington: Ministry of Education.

New Zealand Ministry of Education. (2002). *Pathways to the Future: Ngā Huarahi Arataki. A 10-Year Strategic Plan for Early Childhood Education*. Wellington: Ministry of Education.

New Zealand Ministry of Education. (2004, 2007, 2009). *Kei Tua o te Pae. Assessment for learning: Early Childhood Exemplars*. Wellington: Learning Media.

New Zealand Ministry of Education. (2006). *Ngā Arohaehae Whai Hua—Self-review Guidelines for ECE*. Wellington: Ministry of Education, Learning Media.

New Zealand Ministry of Education. (2008). *Ka Hikitia. Managing for Success. Māori Education Strategy 2008–2012*. Wellington: Ministry of Education.

New Zealand Ministry of Education. (2009). *Te Whatu Pōkeka. Kaupapa Māori Assessment for Learning. Early Childhood Exemplars*. Wellington Learning Media. Retrieved from http://www.educate.ece.govt.nz/~/media/Educate/Files/Reference%20Downloads/TeWhatuPokeka.pdf.

New Zealand Ministry of Education. (2013). *Ka hikitia. Accelerating Success. 2013–2017. The Māori Education Strategy*. Wellington, New Zealand: Ministry of Education. Retrieved from http://www.minedu.govt.nz/theMinistry/PolicyAndStrategy/KaHikitia.aspx.

New Zealand Ministry of Education, & New Zealand Teachers Council. (2011). *Tātaiako: Cultural Competencies for Teachers of Mäori Learners*. Wellington: New Zealand Ministry of Education & New Zealand Teachers Council. Retrieved from http://akoaotearoa.ac.nz/mi/download/ng/file/group-199/a-literature-review-of-kaupapa-maori-and-maori-education-pedagogy.pdf.

Nuttall, J. (2003). Introduction. In J. Nuttall (Ed.), *Weaving Te Whāriki: Aotearoa New Zealand's Early Childhood Curriculum Document in Theory and Practice* (pp. 5–15). Wellington: New Zealand Council for Educational Research.

Nuttall, J. (2005). *Pathway to the Future? Doing Childcare in the Era of New Zealand's Early Childhood Strategic Plan*. Wellington: Institute for Early Childhood Studies. Victoria University of Wellington.

Orange, C. (1987). *The Treaty of Waitangi*. Wellington: Allen and Unwin/Port Nicholson Press.

Papakura, M. (1938/1986). *The Old-time Maori*. Auckland: New Women's Press.

Pere, R. R. (1982/1994). *Ako. Concepts and Learning in the Maori tradition*. Hamilton: Department of Sociology, University of Waikato. Reprinted by Te Kohanga Reo National Trust Board.

Peters, M. A. (2001). *Poststructuralism, Marxism, and Neoliberalism*. Lanham: Rowman & Littlefield.

Piggot-Irvine, E., Aitken, H., Ritchie, J., Bruce Ferguson, P., & McGrath, F. (2009). Induction of newly qualified teachers in New Zealand. *Asia-Pacific Journal of Teacher Education, 37*(2), 175–198.

Policy Strategy and Research Group Department of Corrections. (2007). *Over-representation of Māori in the Criminal Justice System: An Exploratory Report*. Wellington, NZ: Department of Corrections.

Retrieved from http://www.corrections.govt.nz/__data/assets/
pdf_file/0004/285286/Over-representation-of-Maori-in-the-
criminal-justice-system.pdf.

Ritchie, J. (2002). *"It's Becoming Part of Their Knowing": A Study of Bicultural Development in an Early Childhood Teacher Education Setting in Aotearoa/ New Zealand*. PhD thesis. University of Waikato, Hamilton.

Ritchie, J. (2003a). Te Whāriki as a potential lever for bicultural development. In J. Nuttall (Ed.), *Weaving Te Whāriki* (pp. 79–109). Wellington: New Zealand Council for Educational Research.

Ritchie, J. (2003b). *Whakawhanaungatanga: Dilemmas for mainstream New Zealand early childhood education of a commitment to bicultural pedagogy*. Presented as part of panel, Crossing Borders: The Relevance of Cultural Values and Understandings in Our Construction of Quality. Paper presented at the 11th Reconceptualizing Early Childhood Conference, January 5–12, Tempe, Arizona. Retrieved from http://unitec.researchbank.ac.nz/handle/10652/1479.

Ritchie, J. (2005). Implementing Te Whāriki as postmodern practice: a perspective from Aotearoa/New Zealand. In S. Ryan & S. Grieshaber (Eds), *Practical transformations and transformational practices: Globalization, postmodernism, and early childhood education* (Vol. 14, pp. 109–136). Amsterdam: Elsevier.

Ritchie, J. (2013). *Te Whāriki* and the promise of early childhood care and education grounded in a commitment to Te Tiriti o Waitangi. In J. Nuttall (Ed.), *Weaving Te Whāriki* (2nd ed., pp. 141–156). Wellington: NZCER Press.

Ritchie, J., & Johnson, A. (2011). Early childhood care and education. In M. C. Dale, M. O'Brien & S. St. John (Eds), *Left Further Behind: How Policies Fail the Poorest Children in New Zealand* (pp. 159–174). Auckland: Child Poverty Action Group, Inc.

Ritchie, J., & Rau, C. (2006). Whakawhanaungatanga. Partnerships in bicultural development in early childhood education. Final Report to the Teaching & Learning Research Initiative Project. Wellington: Teaching Learning Research Institute/New Zealand Centre for Educational Research. Retrieved from http://www.tlri.org.nz/tlri-research/research-completed/ece-sector/whakawhanaungatanga%E2%80%94-partnerships-bicultural-development.

Robertson, S., & Dale, R. (2009). The World Bank, the IMF, and the possibilities of critical education. In M. Apple, W. W. Au, &

L. A. Gandin (Eds), *The Routledge International Handbook of Critical Education* (pp. 23–35). New York: Routledge.

Roffe, J. (2007). The revolutionary dividual. In A. Hickey-Moody & P. Malins (Eds), *Deleuzian Encounters: Studies in Contemporary Social Issues* (pp. 40–49). Houndmills, Basingstoke, Hampshire, and New York: Palgrave Macmillan.

Rogoff, B. (2003). *The Cultural Nature of Human Development.* Oxford: Oxford University Press.

Salmond, A. (1991). *Two Worlds: First Meetings between Māori and Europeans, 1642–1772.* Auckland: Viking.

Saltman, K. J. (2009). Corporatization and the control of schools. In M. Apple, W. W. Au, & L. A. Gandin (Eds), *The Routledge International Handbook of Critical Education* (pp. 51–63). New York: Routledge.

Simon, J. (1996). Good intentions, but... In R. Steele (Ed.), *Whakamana Tangata* (pp. 38–42). Wellington: Quest Rapuara.

Simon, J. (2000). Education policy change: historical perspectives. In J. Marshall, E. Coxon, K. Jenkins, & A. Jones (Eds), *Politics, Policy, Pedagogy: Education in Aotearoa/New Zealand* (pp. 25–68). Palmerston North: Dunmore.

Smith, L. T. (1995). The colonisation of Māori children. *Youth Law Review, August/September/October*, 8–11.

Stiglitz, J. (2010, 6 April). Meltdown: Not just a metaphor. Vested interests cause both our financial system and the nuclear industry to compulsively underestimate risk. *The Guardian.* Retrieved from http://www.guardian.co.uk/commentisfree/cifamerica/2011/apr/06/japan-nuclearpower.

Te One, S. (2003). The context for Te Whāriki: contemporary issues of influence. In J. Nuttall (Ed.), *Weaving Te Whāriki* (pp. 17–49). Wellington: NZCER.

Waitangi Tribunal. (1999). *The wānanga Capital Establishment Report: Maori Education in New Zealand.* Wellington: Waitangi Tribunal. Retrieved from http://www.waitangi-tribunal.govt.nz/scripts/reports/reports/718/75BF64FC-B0AD-47EE-ADC6-5CF7C764BD0B.pdf.

Walker, R. (2004). *Ka Whawhai Tonu Matou: Struggle without End* (revised ed.). Auckland: Penguin.

6
A Counter-Colonial Pedagogy of Affect in Early Childhood Education in Aotearoa New Zealand

Jenny Ritchie

> **Abstract:** *This chapter takes a theoretical approach inspired by the work of Paulo Freire, Michel Foucault, Giles Deleuze, and Felix Guattari, to reflect upon an assemblage that is constitutive of a series of studies of early childhood practice in Aotearoa, the lens being the facilitation by educators of the involvement and engagement of Māori parents and their children within mainstream early childhood care and education (ECCE) settings. The three studies (Ritchie, Duhn, Rau, & Craw, 2010; Ritchie & Rau, 2006, 2008)[1] were conducted in collaboration with educators committed to implementing the expectations of the ECCE curriculum. These teachers are seen to have generated lines of flight that transgress previously striated spaces, territorialized through colonization, via a pedagogy of affect grounded in kaupapa Māori (Māori philosophy) values.*
>
> Ritchie J., and M. Skerrett. *Early Childhood Education in Aotearoa New Zealand: History, Pedagogy, and Liberation.* New York: Palgrave Macmillan, 2014.
> DOI: 10/1057.9781137375797.0010.

Background

At the time of writing, it is 17 years since the publication of *Te Whāriki*, the ECCE curriculum for Aotearoa New Zealand (New Zealand Ministry of Education, 1996). *Te Whāriki* was radical, revolutionary even, in its socio-cultural, holistic orientation and its validation and inclusion of Indigenous (Māori) epistemology. It posed, and continues to pose, a huge challenge to the largely monocultural ECCE teacher workforce. We have already described in previous chapters of this book this bi-epistemological frame as being based in *Te Tiriti o Waitangi*, the 1840 agreement between the British Crown and Māori Chiefs that allowed for colonial settlement in exchange for upholding the independence of the Chiefs to maintain their lands and other resources in order to sustain their peoples.

The "holistic" integration of the curriculum is seen in explanation of the principle of Holistic Development—Kotahitanga, which affirms that: "Cognitive, social, cultural, physical, emotional, and spiritual dimensions of human development are integrally interwoven" (New Zealand Ministry of Education, 1996, p. 41). Learning and development are to be fostered by ensuring the "recognition of the spiritual dimension of children's lives in culturally, socially, and individually appropriate ways" (p. 41). Under the principle of Empowerment—Whakamana, the curriculum requires that: "Particular care should be given to bicultural issues in relation to empowerment. Adults working with children should understand and be willing to discuss bicultural issues, actively seek Māori contributions to decision making, and ensure that Māori children develop a strong sense of self-worth" (p. 40).

The *Te Whāriki* strand of "Belonging—Mana whenua" is the only strand to focus on both children and their families. It is a key professional responsibility for educators to ensure that "Children and their families feel a sense of belonging" (New Zealand Ministry of Education, 1996, p. 54). The document elaborates further, that "Children and their families [should] experience an environment where: connecting links with the family and the wider world are affirmed and extended; [children and families] know that they have a place; [and] they feel comfortable with the routines, customs, and regular events" (p. 54). It is recognized that this feeling of belonging is paramount to well-being: "The feeling of belonging, in the widest sense, contributes to inner well-being, security, and identity" (p. 54).

The families of all children should feel that they belong and are able to participate in the early childhood education programme and in decision making. Māori and Tagata Pasefika [Pacific Islands peoples] children will be more likely to feel at home if they regularly see Māori and Pacific Islands adults in the early childhood education setting. Liaison with local tangata whenua [Indigenous people, Māori] and a respect for [P]apatuanuku [Earth Mother] should be promoted. (New Zealand Ministry of Education, 1996, p. 54)

This was a significant shift for many ECCE educators in New Zealand, particularly within the teacher-led sector (rather than *whānau*/family and parent-led settings such as Kōhanga Reo and Playcentre), who had previously perceived their role to be one of working with children, rather than engaging more than peripherally with *whānau*/families.

A further interpretation of the implications of *Te Whāriki* is that in 1996, early childhood educators were suddenly cast into the role of cultural workers (Freire, 2005) engaged in education as a "political practice" (Malewski, 2005, p. 72). As cultural workers, educators take steps to come to "know the concrete world in which their students live, the culture in which their students' language, syntax, semantics, and accent are found in action, in which certain habits, likes, beliefs, fears, desires are formed that are not necessarily easily accepted in the teachers' own worlds" (Malewski, 2005, p. 72). Particularly when working with young children, relationships with families form the bridge to gaining deeper insight into the child's habits, likes, beliefs, fears, and desires.

Michel Foucault (1991, 1995) alerted us to the insidious hidden effects of our embodiment within instruments and vectors of power, whereby technologies of power operate through oppressive though often subtly coercive systems of punishment and surveillance. Neoliberalist governmentality allows governments to side-step direct responsibility and accountability for provision of public services, power effects being ostensibly diffused and de-centered via capitalist/corporatist "privatization" under the guise of liberalist individual "freedom" and "choice." Deleuze and Guattari offer ways of dissembling the seductions of the machinations of capitalism, offering considerations of a-centered non-hierarchical rhizomatic mutiplicities (Deleuze & Guattari, 2004). Te Whāriki as an assemblage is constituted through multiple desirings. "The rationality, the efficiency, of an assemblage does not exist without the passions the assemblage brings into play, without the desires that constitute it as much as it constitutes them" (Deleuze & Guattari, 2004,

p. 440). Desire is thus recognized as an intrinsic driver, revolutionary in its pursuit of further connections and assemblages (Deleuze & Parnet, 2002; Tuck, 2010). Teachers can be seen as enablers/dis-ablers of desire(s), via their positioning, which potentially enables them to create spaces that allow for ethical unfoldings of space(s) driven by intrinsic desires for new becomings:

> Drawn together with the concepts of smooth and striated space, the notion of the fold enables an ethical evaluation of space according to the kinds of bodies and social relations it makes possible. Connected to Deleuze's concept of affect, it becomes possible to articulate the ways in which even a small alteration to a socio-spatial assemblage can affect ethico-political changes. (Hickey-Moody & Malins, 2007, p. 12)

In Deleuze-Guattarian thinking, desire is associated with passion, and with lack, or yearning for what is lacking (Deleuze & Guattari, 2004). Affect is seen as a felt "intensity corresponding to the passage from one experiential state of the body to another and implying an augmentation or diminution in that body's capacity to act" (Deleuze & Guattari, 2004, p. xvii). The everyday presence, or becoming-ness, of teachers is in this view a powerful source in service of ethical unfoldings, of pedagogies that are mindful of desirings and affects. In this chapter, I use examples from recent studies (Ritchie et al., 2010; Ritchie & Rau, 2006, 2008) to demonstrate ways in which educators moved into experimenting with new "pedagogies of affect" (Albrecht-Crane & Daryl Slack, 2007); whereby multiplicities of new lines of flight emerged (Deleuze & Parnet, 2002), involving previously un-thought ethical trajectories, the dismantling of former practices, and the emergence of destratifying processes of becoming.

Methodologies

The studies referred to in this chapter (Ritchie et al., 2010; Ritchie & Rau, 2006, 2008) utilized protocols and processes that resonate with kaupapa Māori (Bishop, 2005; Smith, 1999/2012), critical indigenous (Denzin, Lincoln, & Smith, 2008), and narrative (Clandinin, 2007) methodologies. Educators were positioned as co-researchers alongside project co-directors from within the academy. There was a strong methodological intention to gather voices of both parents and children through a variety of methods that included center pedagogical documentation and policy documents; educator reflections; transcripts of interviews with teachers, families, and children; photographs and video; and children's art and narratives. Please go to the original full reports of each study for detailed explanations of the respective methodological processes.

Data examples

In the study *Whakawhanaungatanga: Partnerships in bicultural development in early childhood education* (Ritchie & Rau, 2006), we worked closely with a number of research partners, one of which was an *iwi* (tribal) education initiative, the Hei Ara Kōkiri Tūwharetoa Education Initiative. In our ongoing consultations with representatives of this initiative, we were frequently, gently reminded to widen our lens to proactively ensure the inclusion of *whānau* (families) in our research design, data gathering, analysis, and theorizing. Our languaging was quite often called in to question, when, for example, we used the word "teacher" rather than the more inclusive term "educator." We tried to be ever mindful that our use of particular terminologies reflects Foucaultian hidden power flows, subtly conveying either a disconnection or degrees of connectedness, which, from a Māori perspective is prioritized through values of *whanaungatanga* (family relatedness), *manaakitanga* (caring, hospitality, generosity), and *wairuatanga* (spiritual interconnectedness). These relational expectations resonate within the domain of affect, requiring the upholding of the *mana* (integrity, authority) of each individual as a representative of their *whakapapa* (genealogical connectedness), the "committed sapiential circles" that enfold each member of the collective within its embrace (Mead, 1978, p. xixii).

The data drawn from the collaboration with the Hei Ara Kōkiri Tuwaretoa Education Initiative provided deep insight into the vision and aspirations of *whānau* Māori (Māori families). Their data confirmed previous findings (Else, 1997; Newell, 2000) that examined reasons for the lower participation of Māori children and *whānau* in formal ECCE settings. The concerns that were re-iterated were the prohibitive cost of many services; the monolingualism (English—only spoken); the lack of fluency of teachers in te reo Māori (the Māori language); and the fact that Māori children who did attend these services were receiving very minimal exposure to their language (Ritchie & Rau, 2006). Despite the de/re-territorializing encroachment of colonization/Western globalized discourses, many *whānau* Māori (Māori families) remained and remain resolute in their desire for their children to have access to their language, and that this re-assertion is mandated by *Te Tiriti o Waitangi* and *Te Whāriki* to be included in "mainstream"/"whitestream" (alongside Māori-immersion specific) government-funded ECCE provision (New Zealand Ministry of Education, 2013; Ritchie, 2008).

The "aspiration statement" from *Te Whāriki* is viewed by many as foundational to the curriculum (Alvestad, Duncan, & Berge, 2009; Lee, Carr, Soutar, & Mitchell, 2013). Yet the statement could be critiqued as being rather individualistic, and contextually deficient in its view that children should be supported "to grow up as competent and confident learners and communicators, healthy in mind, body, and spirit, secure in their sense of belonging and in the knowledge that they make a valued contribution to society" (New Zealand Ministry of Education, 1996, p. 9). A respondent in the data contributed by the Hei Ara Kōkiri Tūwharetoa Education Initiative provided this alternative iteration of an aspiration for all children in Aotearoa: "I would like to see our tamariki [children] being bilingual and being completely comfortable in either Māori or Pākehā settings—having an understanding of the protocols or expected behaviour in these, i.e., bicultural" (as cited in Ritchie & Rau, 2006, p. 24). This upholds a desire for the honouring of Māori language, culture, and people as might have been expected if the assurances articulated in *Te Tiriti o Waitangi* had not been dismantled by layers of colonization (Ritchie, 2013).

In the next study "*Te Puawaitanga—Partnerships with tamariki and whānau in bicultural early childhood care and education*" (Ritchie & Rau, 2008), the teachers of Richard Hudson Kindergarten in Dunedin, in the South Island of New Zealand, provided in-depth data including interviews with parents of some of their children. Here is an excerpt from their data:

> Our reflections to support the data for Kiyana
>
> Kiyana is a four-and-a-half-year-old girl who attends morning sessions at Richard Hudson Kindergarten. She has a natural inclination to things Māori, and is a very able child. We believe that commitment and daily practice of integrating te reo and tikanga Māori [Māori language and culture] is very visible and supports our kaupapa [philosophy]—through Kiyana's keen response to new kupu [Māori words] when she is excited to transfer this to home—this is the principle whānau tangata [Family and Community Principle from Te Whāriki] in action, it also shows the tuakana–teina [older sibling/child supporting younger] strategy where she is the competent person sharing new info with others and helping them to

this competency. We also celebrate the concept ako [learning/teaching], where the role of teaching and learning is reciprocal, Kiyana is the teacher with the new kupu [words].

Kiyana constantly seeks new contextual kupu [words] to stretch and challenge her learning. This, we view as self-assessment and is key to intrinsic motivation, building on her competence and confidence, knowing that she is a learner capable of adding to the knowledge she has, and knowing that she is constantly learning more. She is keen to ask for a new kupu, and if the adult she asks doesn't know, she is learning how that adult may seek answers from another adult or look it up in the dictionary. We believe that this reflects that Kiyana feels valued with her learning, we take her seriously and she knows this. When we don't know an answer, we are honest and say "I don't know" and together go off to find out. We see the glee in her eye when she asks us questions we don't know the answers to—authenticity is alive in our practice.

We know that she is proud of these accomplishments and know that the principle of whakamana [Te Whāriki Principle of Empowerment] is also enacted in our daily practice for her to demonstrate this. Seeing Kiyana with this thirst for challenge and extension is like "life blood" to teachers who are also keen to keep passionate about delivering on a treaty-based curriculum [referring to Te Tiriti o Waitangi aspirations].

This further supports the information originally sent about the interview with Kiyana's parents (Kelly and Warren May 25th) where Warren is feeling affirmed as a generation who missed the opportunity to live and learn his native tongue, his excitement and celebration of Kiyana's new learning is welcomed and implemented into their family context. We see him as proud and willing to learn alongside his daughter, who is actively participating in reo in the kindergarten context. We believe this is non-threatening for Warren because we as teachers are non-Māori but supported by Māori resource teachers, so again the community of learners is embraced and practiced without anyone feeling whakamā [shy/embarrassed]. We also believe that the [Te Whāriki] principle ngā hononga/relationships has been a key to this success as we have a relaxed and friendly relationship with this family which has enabled a non-threatening approach to building on reo together. (as cited in Ritchie & Rau, 2008, pp. 108–111)

In this excerpt of narrative data provided by the teachers of Richard Hudson Kindergarten, the teachers' philosophy, guided by the early childhood curriculum *Te Whāriki*, means that they are consciously visibilizing Māori language and cultural practices, enacted through deeply engaged relationships with children and their families. This conscious, deliberate process of revisibilizing *te ao* Māori destratifies the rigidity of monocultural discourses, creating an affordance for Kiyana whereby she feels a strong desire to access *kupu* Māori. This line of flight is enhanced for Kiyana through the synergy that she experiences between home and center. Meanwhile, her father Warren, who was denied access to his language and culture in the formerly striated monocultural education system, celebrates his daughter's passion for their language. Kiyana has found her kindergarten to be a space that welcomes her discovery of her ancestral knowledges. She is able to unfold her "relations with the world" as the kindergarten program unfurls "the categories of identity and habit" that enable access to widened possibilities for identity positionings (Hickey-Moody & Malins, 2007, p. 12). Kiyana is embarked upon a line of flight enabling "change and metamorphosis" (Woodward, 2007) for herself and her family. Such lines of flight are "instantiations of desire, the primal force upon which society is built. As such, they form a productive, affirmative, and positive dynamism pointing to the nexus of change" (Albrecht-Crane & Daryl Slack, 2007, p. 102).

In the same study (Ritchie & Rau, 2008), the teachers of Maungatapu kindergarten in the North Island city of Tauranga also interviewed several parents for the project, including Josie, a Māori parent, who had a long-standing involvement with their center:

TEACHER: It would be valuable to hear your thoughts on how things look and feel in this environment since our last discussion. Have you noticed any changes?

JOSIE: I have noticed that with the teachers' use of Te Reo it is being used more regularly, I am hearing it more through conversation. You have become more comfortable and it's at a point now where it's just a part of you. The children understand the language and their understanding is clearer. They aren't threatened by it, it is normal, a normal part of the kindy. With the mirimiri [Māori therapeutic massage], I noticed with the children and even with the teachers ... Māori have a holistic point of view of touch and the children were at first unsure of it but I noticed that they became more and more comfortable. Some of them said, "No I don't want to do that but they ended up participating because they realized that they were going to massage themselves. They understand they are responsible for their body, their tinana. I also noticed that this environment is non-threatening. I noticed even this morning how quickly the children picked up the actions when we were singing and they were really enjoying it so incorporating that as well and singing is part of the Māori way of life, music and dance and they love it. It actually blows me away because I have seen big changes but it has been very gently introduced, the changes haven't been forced they have just become ... integrated.

TEACHER: The children have naturally taken it on board and I find they have naturally just accepted it and run with and are enjoying being a part of this environment. It has become a part of the culture of the kindergarten.
JOSIE: And that's what Māori is. It's just a lifestyle and it's about being aware of body, mind, spirit, soul, emotion and children go away with the confidence of knowing who they are and it doesn't have to be tied to one culture.
TEACHER: I think the children are using more Te Reo. Have you heard them using the language during your work here?
JOSIE: They are and they are more aware of it. It's not just in the way they speak it's in their actions as well and it's very, very clear.
TEACHER: In what way. What are you seeing?
JOSIE: Well even in their interactions with each other like at mat time and it's like an awareness ... The whole environment of the kindy and what's happening has become very normal.
TEACHER: What changes have you seen since Danielle left to go to school? Our last conversation was just before she went to school and you talked a lot about the feeling of the place.
JOSIE: Yeah the feeling ...
TEACHER: Has that changed for you or is it the same?
JOSIE: Well my perspective has changed as I was a parent but coming in and working alongside the children and for me the feeling is one of oneness. There is a feeling of oneness and belonging and regardless of whether Danielle is at school or not the feeling of belonging is there and that's wonderful. You can pat yourselves on the back because I guess in your own ways you have changed—you have all been open to this growth.
TEACHER: Well I guess it has been so interesting for us as we love learning about different cultures and different languages. I think we are lucky that we can integrate different cultures into our kindergarten. The children all come on board and we have learnt together.
JOSIE: Children I think take things on board. As adults we often put things in the too hard basket but children they just want to do it.
TEACHER: I've really enjoyed learning the weaving, the massage and the benefits of it and having the wharenui [meeting house] and learning some of the terminologies surrounding it such as the tukutuku [woven] panels, the whakapapa [genealogy] panels in there and it's interesting learning alongside the children.
JOSIE: And ... with the children ... their perception of yourselves Marion, Debbie and Jude that's fantastic ... The privilege that knowing that because ... you are the kaiako [teachers], because of you ... that they can do what they do. The wharenui represents who you are. It's a place of learning and you have incorporated so many things in this place of learning and children can evolve or go off to school and then they are like Danielle and want to come back, which is

understandable. It's such a different environment for them and I guess they realise the freedom of expression and being able to do things at their pace, in their time and learn to their abilities changes when they go to school.

Josie, a Māori mother, has felt comfortable and included within the kindergarten program, where the teachers are predominately *Pākehā* (of European ancestry). Furthermore, she has observed the teachers becoming more comfortable themselves, in their increasing, inclusive delivery of *te reo* and *te ao* Māori (Māori language and worldview). Josie encourages the teachers to celebrate their growth, as demonstrated by the "wonderful feeling of oneness and belonging" that she senses in the kindergarten. Josie highlights how, from her *te ao* Māori perspective, "body, mind, spirit, soul, and emotion" are integrated within education (and other) enactment, and furthermore, that this is a source of emotional and spiritual well-being that upholds the *mana* (integrity, esteem) of both *tamariki* Māori (Māori children) and the wider collective of all members (teachers, children, family members) of the kindergarten community. In addition to the more common inclusion of Māori songs and action dances, *mirimiri* (traditional Māori massage) has become an accepted part of the kindergarten program, the therapeutic benefits of touch a multi-sensorial, embodied source of well-being enhancement. The skill of these teachers as cultural workers is evident, as changes to strengthen the *te ao* Māori content have been introduced gently and respectfully over time to the point that *te ao* Māori now resonates within the everyday enactment of children. Josie recognizes the proactive modelling of these *Pākehā* "*kaiako*" (teachers of European ancestry) as leading this transformative process. She affirms the symbolic value of the *wharenui* (Māori meeting house) that has been collaboratively created at the kindergarten, seeing it as representing the strength of the teachers' commitment to *te ao* Māori. The respectful dynamics evident in this interview are representative of a pedagogical enactment of *Tiriti o Waitangi* founded praxis. The sense of *whanaungatanga* (relationships) established within this kindergarten is profound and enduring.

Later in the project Marion Dekker, the Head Kindergarten teacher at Maungatapu Kindergarten, offered the following reflection:

> An interesting comment that one of our Pākehā mothers through the interview was saying how wonderful and warm and welcoming and inclusive the place was and she said, "Tell me is that because you are trying really strongly to deliver a bicultural programme here in this kindergarten,

or is that because it's *you* guys?" And we found it interesting to stop and think—"Okay, now is this about our personalities? Is this *who we are?*" and after lots of discussion I was excited and kind of encouraged to be able to say to the team, "Yes there's an openness there and that openness people recognise as an embracing and that actually we want to know who you are, we want to share who you are and this is *who we are.*" Yes it's kind of a dovetailing of a person who's growing and is open and is understanding and is inclusive, but it's also that person has embraced an understanding and is trying to represent that in a way that is visible not only on the walls, but is visible in life. Actually it's not about who I am, it's because *I'm committed* to delivering that, and so I will behave like this to do that and I will reflect like this to do that and that's what the spin-off has been in our team is that when we're looking at self-review on any aspect of the programme or the routines or the happenings or what's happening in the kindergarten and all aspects of it, it is now a question that's always asked: "How will this impact on Māori? How will this impact on how we will deliver this? What will we need to say about that?" And I'm not saying that we're good at that yet, but I'm excited to say that actually now my team think about that and so I think that's been a shift for us, and I have seen growth in the way the team welcome new Māori families that come into kindergarten, and so that's really encouraging for me to see, because they are growing. (as cited in Ritchie & Rau, 2008, p. 65)

At Maungatapu Kindergarten, the collective of teachers, under the leadership of Head Teacher Marion, are also modelling a shift away from striated spaces. A sense of "nomadic subjectivity" enables these teachers "to move across conventional categories and move against 'settled' concepts and theories," offering incitement to shift beyond their previous boundaries and comfort zones (Sellers & Gough, 2010, p. 598). The unfoldings described in the Maungatapu data above demonstrate the "intensive potentiality which is embedded (or enfolded) within any body or space: a propensity—or virtual intensity—generated by the folding in of matter which, given the right conditions, has the capacity to unfold" (Malins, 2007, p. 158). As Māori ways of "knowing, being, and doing" (Martin, 2007; New Zealand Ministry of Education, 2009) become re-normalized (Smith, 1999/2012) within their program, it seems that these teachers' openness to and insight regarding the nomadic positionings of both themselves and of *whānau* Māori (Māori families) has invited the collective of teachers, parents, and children of their center "to see the ordinary extra-ordinarily and to see-think-write-picture differently" (Sellers & Gough, 2010, p. 598).

The third study, "Titiro Whakamuri, Hoki Whakamua. We are the future, the present and the past: caring for self, others and the environment in early years' teaching and learning" (Ritchie et al., 2010) extended on the previous two projects (Ritchie & Rau, 2006, 2008). The focus of this particular project again drew upon kaupapa Māori (Māori philosophy), applying it this time more specifically, to "caring for ourselves, each other and the environment." A pedagogy of affect was thus applied to caring for Papatūānuku (Earth Mother and Ranginui (Sky Father) through the sharing of Māori cosmologies that enabled children (and families) to re-connect with the source of our sustenance and well-being. Being and working with(in) the more-than-human world (Abram, 1996; Plumwood, 2002) through ongoing regular activities such as gardening, caring for ECCE center pets, and beach clean-up walks became a strong focus within the participating settings, kaupapa Māori (Māori philosophy) understandings deepening the sense of connectedness, as seen in these examples:

> Papatūānuku (Earth Mother) and Ranginui (Sky Father) look after all of us. The sun, wind, rain and air look after the plants that look after us. We are nurturing our tamariki [children] to look after their environment. In caring for our natural environment, the tamariki are developing respectful relationships with nature whilst nurturing their health, wellbeing and wairua (spirituality/soul) within. The children freely interact with our garden to express their inner thoughts and emotions. Sadly, we lost our pet rabbit, Misty. The children miss our pet rabbit and often pick flowers from our garden or theirs and lay them on the ground by Misty. [Hawera Kindergarten].

> Our little pot plants had finished flowering so we recycled them by transplanting succulents in the pots. First we had karakia [prayer, blessing] to acknowledge Tāne Mahuta [departmental god, spiritual guardian of forests, plants, insects and birds], then broke off pieces of the succulent plants, sat them in the pots and watered them. The children carried river stones from the gravel pit and poured them into the planter boxes. We talked about gardening, looking after the plants, where the stones came from and experienced the mauri (life force) in the plants and stones. It was a good team effort. When we had finished, the children admired their work. When one works with Papatūānuku, one can find it relaxing and peaceful. It teaches patience and nurtures the soul. [Hawera Kindergarten]

> If we hadn't had the challenge of bringing in a Māori component to the project, it just would never have had the depth, the emotion, the identity and the wholeness that weaving te Ao Māori [the Māori world] has accorded. [Richard Hudson Kindergarten]

These excerpts portray the sense of *wairuatanga*, spiritual interconnectedness, underpinning the work by these teachers and children, and recognition of interdependence with(in) and reliance upon the more-than-human world. This recognition is not necessarily articulated verbally, but comes through embodied, sensory engagement in the regular daily work of *kaitiakitanga* (active guardianship, stewardship, and care-taking).

Conclusion

Retrospective re-theorizing of recent research reports can enable new understandings and enhanced respect for the complexities of the work of teachers who engage in the deep ethical work of de-colonizing transformation. Whilst acknowledging the historicity of ECCE as a mechanism for social regulation and colonialism (May, 1997), we see new lines of flight and becomings being made available by teachers, children, and their families, through a reciprocity of engagement, a pedagogy of affect (Albrecht-Crane & Daryl Slack, 2007).The teachers whose work has been touched upon in the above extracts, through their desire for ethical unfoldings and connection in their practice, are seen to have generated lines of flight that transgress previously striated spaces, destabilizing historically ingrained patterns of colonization, through these pedagogies of affect (Albrecht-Crane & Daryl Slack, 2007; Deleuze & Parnet, 2002; Hickey-Moody & Malins, 2007).

Enactment incited by the bi-epistemological frame of *Te Whāriki* is enabling new multiplicities of assemblage(s), of lines of flight that are re-tracing "of the world present, past and future" (Deleuze & Guattari, 2004, p. 26). Despite recent calls for it to be reviewed, *Te Whāriki* has so far eluded potential reterritorializing by our current government, whose neoliberal philosophy has already eroded a number of key areas related to ethical, high-quality culturally responsive practice (Ritchie, 2012).

> *Where else but in wide expanses and in major upheavals in those expanses, could a tiny rivulet of intensity start to flow?* (Deleuze & Guattari, 2004, p. 38)

Note

1   The first two projects were directed by Jenny Ritchie and Cheryl Rau and in the third project we were joined by two further co-directors, Iris Duhn

and Janita Craw. We acknowledge with gratitude the funding of our projects by the New Zealand Teaching and Learning Research Initiative (TLRI). Summary and full reports of the studies are available on the TLRI website: http://www.tlri.org.nz/tlri-research/research-completed/ece-sector

References

Abram, D. (1996). *The Spell of the Sensuous: Perception and Language in a More-than-Human World*. New York: Vintage Books.

Albrecht-Crane, C., & Daryl Slack, J. (2007). Toward a pedagogy of affect. In A. Hickey-Moody & P. Malins (Eds), *Deleuzian Encounters: Studies in Contemporary Social Issues* (pp. 99–110). Houndmills, Basingstoke, Hampshire, and New York: Palgrave Macmillan.

Alvestad, M., Duncan, J., & Berge, A. (2009). New Zealand ECE teachers talk about Te Whāriki. *Journal of Teachers' Work*, 6(1), 3–19.

Bishop, R. (2005). Freeing ourselves from neocolonial domination in research: A Kaupapa Māori approach to creating knowledge. In N. K. Denzin & Y. S. Lincoln (Eds), *The Sage Handbook of Qualitative Research* (3rd ed., pp. 109–164). Thousand Oaks, California: Sage.

Clandinin, D. J. (Ed.). (2007). *Handbook of Narrative Inquiry: Mapping a Methodology*. Thousand Oaks, California: Sage.

Deleuze, G., & Guattari, F. (2004). *A Thousand Plateaus: Capitalism and Schizophrenia* (B. Massumi, Trans.). London & New York: Continuum.

Deleuze, G., & Parnet, C. (2002). *Dialogues II*. London & New York: Continuum.

Denzin, N. K., Lincoln, Y. S., & Smith, Linda Tuhiwai. (2008). *Handbook of Critical and Indigenous Methodologies*. Los Angeles: Sage.

Else, A. (1997). *Maori Participation & Performance in Education. A Literature Review and Research Programme*. Wellington, New Zealand: Ministry of Education.

Foucault, M. (1991). *The Foucault Reader. An Introduction to Foucault's Thought*. (P. Rabinow, Ed.). London: Penguin.

Foucault, M. (1995). *Discipline and punish. The birth of the prison*. London: Vintage Books.

Freire, P. (2005). *Teachers as Cultural Workers: Letters to Those Who Dare Teach*. Boulder, Colorado: Westview Press.

Hickey-Moody, A., & Malins, P. (2007). Introduction: Gilles Deleuze and four movements in social thought. In A. Hickey-Moody & P. Malins (Eds), *Deleuzian Encounters: Studies in Contemporary Social Issues* (pp. 1–24). Houndmills, Basingstoke, Hampshire, and New York: Palgrave Macmillan.

Lee, W., Carr, M., Soutar, B., & Mitchell, L. (2013). *Understanding the Te Whāriki Approach: Early Years Education in Practice.* London: Routledge.

Malewski, E. (2005). Epilogue: when children and youth talk back. Precocious research practices and the cleverist voices. In L. D. Soto & B. B. Swadener (Eds), *Power & Voice in Research with Children* (pp. 215–222). New York: Peter Lang.

Malins, P. (2007). City folds: injecting drug use and urban space. In A. Hickey-Moody & P. Malins (Eds), *Deleuzian Encounters: Studies in Contemporary Social Issues* (pp. 151–168). Houndmills, Basingstoke, Hampshire, and New York: Palgrave Macmillan.

Martin, K. (2007). Making tracks and reconceptualising Aboriginal early childhood education: an Aboriginal Australian perspective. *Childrenz Issues, 11*(1), 15–20.

May, H. (1997). *The Discovery of Early Childhood.* Auckland: Bridget Williams Books, Auckland University Press.

Mead, M. (1978). Foreword. In J. Ritchie & J. Ritchie (Eds), *Growing up in New Zealand* (pp. ix–xii). Sydney: George Allen & Unwin.

New Zealand Ministry of Education. (1996). Te Whāriki. He whāriki mātauranga mō ngā mokopuna o Aotearoa: Early childhood curriculum. Wellington: Learning Media. Retrieved from http://www.educate.ece.govt.nz/~/media/Educate/Files/Reference%20Downloads/whariki.pdf.

New Zealand Ministry of Education. (2009). *Te Whatu Pōkeka. Kaupapa Māori assessment for learning: Early Childhood Exemplars.* Wellington Learning Media. Retrieved from http://www.educate.ece.govt.nz/~/media/Educate/Files/Reference%20Downloads/TeWhatuPokeka.pdf.

New Zealand Ministry of Education. (2013). *Me Kōrero. Let's Talk. Summary of Online Feedback.* Wellington: New Zealand Ministry of Education. Retrieved from http://www.minedu.govt.nz/theMinistry/PolicyAndStrategy/KaHikitia/MeKoreroLetsTalk.aspx/?moe-tile.

Newell, J. (2000). *Disparities between Maori and Non-Maori Participation in Early Childhood Services in New Zealand.* Monitoring and Evaluation

Research Associates Limited, Wellington for Te Puni Kokiri (the Ministry of Maori Development).

Plumwood, V. (2002). *Environmental Culture: The Ecological Crisis of Reason*. London and New York: Routledge.

Ritchie, J. (2008). Honouring Māori subjectivities within early childhood education in Aotearoa. *Contemporary Issues in Early Childhood*, 9(3), 202–210.

Ritchie, J. (2012). *Recent Changes in Policy Affecting the Early Childhood Care and Education Sector in Aotearoa. Power, Policy and Praxis—A Panel Discussion*. Paper presented at the NZARE Annual Conference, Novotel, Hamilton, November 28–30.

Ritchie, J. (2013). *Te Whāriki* and the promise of early childhood care and education grounded in a commitment to Te Tiriti o Waitangi. In J. Nuttall (Ed.), *Weaving Te Whāriki* (2nd ed., pp. 141–156). Wellington: NZCER Press.

Ritchie, J., Duhn, I., Rau, C., & Craw, J. (2010). Titiro Whakamuri, Hoki Whakamua. We are the future, the present and the past: Caring for self, others and the environment in early years' teaching and learning. Final Report for the Teaching and Learning Research Initiative. Wellington: Teaching and Learning Research Initiative/New Zealand Centre for Educational Research. Retrieved from http://www.tlri.org.nz/tlri-research/research-completed/ece-sector/titiro-whakamuri-hoki-whakamua-we-are-future-present-and.

Ritchie, J, & Rau, C. (2006). Whakawhanaungatanga. Partnerships in bicultural development in early childhood education. Final Report to the Teaching & Learning Research Initiative Project. Wellington: Teaching Learning Research Institute/New Zealand Centre for Educational Research. Retrieved from http://www.tlri.org.nz/tlri-research/research-completed/ece-sector/whakawhanaungatanga%E2%80%94-partnerships-bicultural-development.

Ritchie, J., & Rau, C. (2008). Te Puawaitanga—Partnerships with tamariki and whānau in bicultural early childhood care and education. Final Report to the Teaching Learning Research Initiative. Wellington: Teaching Learning Research Institute/New Zealand Centre for Educational Research. Retrieved from http://www.tlri.org.nz/tlri-research/research-completed/ece-sector/te-puawaitanga-partnerships-tamariki-and-wh%C4%81nau.

Sellers, W., & Gough, N. (2010). Sharing outsider thinking: thinking (differently) with Deleuze in educational philosophy and curriculum inquiry. *International Journal of Qualitative Studies in Education*, 23(5), 589–614.

Smith, L. T. (1999/2012). *Decolonizing Methodologies: Research and Indigenous Peoples*. London and Dunedin: Zed Books Ltd. and University of Otago Press.

Tuck, E. (2010). Breaking up with Deleuze: Desire and valuing the irreconcilable. *International Journal of Qualitative Studies in Education*, 23(5), 635–650.

Woodward, E. (2007). Deleuze and suicide. In A. Hickey-Moody & P. Malins (Eds), *Deleuzian Encounters: Studies in Contemporary Social Issues* (pp. 62–75). Houndmills: Palgrave Macmillan.

Liberatory Praxis: Conclusions

Mere Skerrett and Jenny Ritchie

Ritchie J., and M. Skerrett. *Early Childhood Education in Aotearoa New Zealand: History, Pedagogy, and Liberation.* New York: Palgrave Macmillan, 2014.
DOI: 10.1057/9781137375797.0011.

> Nā te Kōhanga Reo te hōpara makaurangi manu whakatau i rere
>
> *It is through the language nests of Kōhanga Reo that the lead birds are nurtured to navigate from fore and aft, to lead from the front and rear, creating the slipstreams in which the Māori language can survive and thrive.*

Colonization and Linguafaction

Part A of this book foregrounds some of the inherent racist underpinnings of colonization entrenched in the New Zealand consciousness; that consciousness which feeds the racist colonial thinking and narrative that is played out daily through the institutions, throughout the country's media, and in early years' education settings and schools. It is manifest in unequal power relations. No more apparent is this than in the interactions between (colonial-minded) monolingual English-speaking teachers and Indigenous children in their respective education contexts. That our current education system is inherently racist has been well-documented over the intervening years since it was established under the Education Ordinance, 1847, and, it is argued here, reeks of linguafaction: the process by which indigenous languages are wrestled away from indigenous peoples, and from their landscapes. Linguafaction is the language/land disconnect that makes territorialized space unsafe for Indigenous people and their languages (see Chapter 1). The discourse analysis of Chapter 1 is designed to unsettle settler historiographies in Aotearoa/New Zealand, dehegemonize the system, and challenge the one-sided partnerships that developed through the Courts as they undermined the founding documents that allowed for British settlement: the 1835 Declaration of Independence and the 1840 Treaty of Waitangi.

Systemic change

It has long been the case that there have been calls for the education system in Aotearoa/New Zealand to step up, but there are some fundamental steps that the Crown has failed to take—the major one being that the Treaty of Waitangi designed a relationship of rangatiratanga for Māori and kawanatanga for the Crown (see Chapter 2). Having established that the health of *te reo* Māori (Māori language) remains fragile at best, the Waitangi Tribunal (Waitangi Tribunal, 2010) turned to consider the Treaty interests and simply questioned whether the principles of the Treaty can ever be achieved if there is not a recognized place for the language of one of the partners to that Treaty. Simply put, there is a Crown obligation to take what steps are reasonable to assist in the preservation of *te reo* Māori. It must see Māori and *te reo* as not somehow external to itself, but a part of the society it represents—and thus a key influence over how society (through its institutions) conducts itself. Further, the Crown in 2010 endorsed the United Nations Declaration on the Rights of Indigenous Peoples (United Nations, 2007). The Waitangi Tribunal argued for adequate resources to be made available to implement policies so that there is no gap between the rhetoric (Māori language as officially recognized in law) and the reality (Māori language as marginalized in education). The Tribunal asserted: The Crown must therefore recognize that the Māori interest in the language is not the same as the interest of any minority group in New Zealand society in its own language. Accordingly, in decision-making about resource allocation, *te reo* Māori is entitled to a "reasonable degree of preference" and must receive a level of funding in accord with this status (Waitangi Tribunal, 2010, p. 52).

The perennial failure of Māori in the colonial education context creates societal stratifications, positioning Māori as deficit in a foreign knowledge system employing pedagogies of erosion and erasure—that is territorialization. As territorialization disconnects languages, revernacularization of those languages provides a way of reconnecting Indigenous people with their stories, their identities and their cultures. Revernacularization of *te reo* Māori underpins decolonization and dehegemonizes our systems. It is this fundamental that drives the Māori bilingual/immersion movement and underpins Kaupapa Māori practice. *Te reo* Māori has been incorporated into municipal law. It is time to fully incorporate it into municipal practice. Whilst this may be implied in many of the government policies and strategies, the relationship of language to land, to cultural identities, to what it means to be a "New Zealander" has to be made explicit and more than implied. This has consequential implications for teachers and teacher education. It is asserted here that every teacher in Aotearoa, New Zealand must be able to speak the Indigenous Māori language. Anything else supports the ongoing colonial structures and puts *te reo* Māori at further risk in spite of the rhetoric.

Māori language narratives

Rushkoff (2013) in his recent book *Present Shock* discusses the here and now of the neoliberal world that has arrived in a disposable consumer economy where one-click ordering is more important than the actual product being purchased. He asserts that there has been a larger societal shift away from future expectations to current value, and that when people stop looking at the future, they start looking at the present. Coming out of World War II, America's frontier was less about finding new territory to exploit and more about inventing new technologies, which have gone viral. Those technologies have influenced the way we think and our narratives. He argues that multitasking brains are actually incapable of storage of sustained argument because of the impact of those technologies. He calls the phenomenon of living in the here and now "presentism" in our drive to be liberated from twentieth century dangerously compelling ideological narratives; no longer are we convinced that the brutal means are justified by the mythological ends. But along with the "presentism" there is the caution around the events of what he calls narrative collapse. Rushkoff quotes Mark Turner's conclusions, that "Narrative imagining—story—is the fundamental instrument of thought. Rational capacities depend on it. It is our chief means of looking into the future, of predicting, of planning, and of explaining" (2013, p. 13). Narratives provide a foothold, a fixed position from which we reflect and look forward. Further, drawing on Le Guin's observations that story-telling "is one of the basic tools invented by the human mind, for the purpose of gaining understanding. There have been great societies that did not use the wheel, but there have been no societies that did not tell stories" (p. 13), he argues that experiencing the world as a series of stories or narratives is what helps to create the contexts of our lives. This book has argued that it is time for a new story, of counter-colonial re-narrativization of early childhood care and education pedagogies, opening up spaces which re-position Māori stories at the centre.

Māori language narratives as curriculum

Ballara (1986) argued that when children hear *te reo* Māori utilized by a variety of media platforms; when they see it adequately taught as a respected and important part of the curriculum; when they identify it to be a language of prestige and *mana*; and when they know it to be the language used at all levels to discuss wider socio-historical, political, and economic issues, then societal transformation occurs. As linguafaction creates factions and barriers (in the past Māori children found it increasingly harder to verbalize their experiences of school and the wider world through their mother-tongues), Māori language re-generation is enabling (children can re-interpret and verbalize their worlds through their ancestral language and thought). It allows different stories to be told. It provides the tools of critique—making it possible to consider other likelihoods. When the intergenerational transmission of *te reo* Māori is ensured, then language shift (from Māori to English) will have ceased, linguafaction eliminated. *Te Whāriki* (New Zealand Ministry of Education, 1996), in its embryonic state, cannot afford to remain a tokenistic gesture. When Māori/English bilingualism is fully endorsed for the nation's children then Aotearoa will have finally lived up to its Treaty responsibilities and obligations. The deterritorialized spaces will have become fertile grounds for the advancement of *te reo* Māori—and *Te Whāriki* can finally take flight. From the perspectives that have been put forward in this book, the importance of reclaiming indigenous stories, Māori narratives, is the essence of what defines quality in education for New Zealand learners. It is in Kōhanga Reo that the kiwi-feathered cloak is woven. Kōhanga Reo is to be cherished. It is stated that all learners in Aotearoa/New Zealand should have access to, and participate in, high-quality Māori language early learning; that is, Māori language should be a part of the core curriculum in early years' education and beyond. This has implications for all who want to be teachers in Aotearoa/New Zealand and gives expression to the idea espoused in the *Ka Hikitia* strategy (New Zealand Ministry of Education, 2013) that it is Māori language that is what defines us as a unique culture and identity.

Shifting the "whitestream"

Enrollments in Kōhanga Reo have declined markedly over the past 15 years (Waitangi Tribunal, 2010). In 2011, 21 percent (8,916 Māori children) of Māori enrollments in early childhood care and education (ECCE) services were in Kōhanga Reo (New Zealand Ministry of Education, 2011). This means two things for the ECCE sector. Firstly, urgent steps need to be taken towards strengthening the provision within ngā Kōhanga Reo through increasing the numbers of qualified teachers who are fluent in te reo Māori (Waitangi Tribunal, 2010). Secondly, there is surely a huge expectation that the rest of the sector, where the remaining 79 percent of Māori children attend, take very seriously the need to deepen the currently uneven delivery of *te reo* and *te ao* Māori (Māori language and worldviews). This mandate not only comes from *Te Tiriti o Waitangi* obligations and the expectations of *Te Whāriki* but is also the aspiration of *whānau* Māori (Māori families) for their children's education (Dixon, Widdowson, Meagher-Lundberg, McMurchy-Pilkington, & McMurchy-Pilkington, 2007; Robertson, Gunn, Lanumata, & Pryor, 2007).

Currently only 9.1 percent of the total of 20,644 teachers in the early childhood education (ECE) workforce are Māori (Ministry of Education, 2012a). Whilst 24 percent of Māori reported in the previous population census that they were speakers of the Māori language, only 1.6 percent of *Pākehā* (those of European ancestry) responded that they could speak Māori (Statistics New Zealand. Tatauranga Aotearoa, 2010). High-quality models of language are required for language learning, rather than token, minimal, limited amounts. As a research participant made clear:

> Teachers and children need to be using dialogue to work with each other—co-constructing. In order to reflect this, we need to provide environments rich in Māori language. We need proficient speaking Māori teachers! Regurgitating learnt phrases will not provide the opportunities for children to really conscientise their experiences, that is, thinking in Māori. Only a very high level of exposure in Māori will do that. (previously unpublished data from the Whakawhanaungatanga study, Ritchie & Rau, 2006)

Pre-service teacher education has an important role to play in shifting the expectations and competencies of beginning teachers to a higher level of (bi)cultural competency, which raises question-marks about current New Zealand government policy to shift primary and secondary teacher education programs from the current situation of predominately three-year bachelors' degrees, to one-year post-graduate level courses, without requiring that the pre-requisite under-graduate program specializes in education, or *te reo* Māori. Whilst the scope of three-year programs of initial teacher education may not be long enough to develop in graduates a high degree of proficiency in the Māori language, it is long enough to foster an understanding of, and commitment to, the key professional responsibilities outlined in *Te Whāriki, Ka Hikitia*, and other ministry documents, in relation to the expectation to deliver high-quality (culturally responsive) Tiriti-based ECCE programs (Ministry of Education, 2012b). The shift to post-graduate primary and secondary teaching qualifications will position ECE teachers at a lower level of qualification than those in the compulsory sector. Parity for early childhood educators has been a long-standing struggle in this country. Yet, if the ECCE sector wants to maintain parity of qualification levels, it would be very difficult for non-Māori teacher education students to attain the cultural competencies espoused in *"Tātaiako"* in a one-year time-frame. Mentoring of beginning teachers, and regular opportunities for relevant in-service professional learning are important factors that contribute to teacher competence (Aitken, Piggot-Irvine, Bruce Ferguson, McGrath, & Ritchie, 2008; Piggot-Irvine, Aitken, Ritchie, Bruce Ferguson, & McGrath, 2009).

Whilst the individualism of neoliberalism directly contravenes the collectivism of te ao Māori, as expressed through Māori values of *whanaungatanga* (relationships, connectedness), *aroha* (the reciprocal obligation to care, respect), *utu* (reciprocity), *manaakitanga* (generosity), and *kaitiakitanga* (guardianship of the earth), Deleuze-Guatarrain thought suggests a mode of ethical resistance to such regimes. Ethical possibilities at the teacher/inter-intra personal/pedagogical interface might include dispositions of sensitivity, humility, reflexivity, and compassion (*manaakitanga*), grounded in acknowledgment of the centrality of culture(s) to identities and learning. Furthermore, in shifting away from monocultural/Western-dominated pedagogies, an openness to and respect for Māori culture extends to the inclusion of the home cultures of all those attending a center, since *kaupapa* Māori values require the enactment of *manaakitanga* (caring, generosity, and hospitality) to all ethnicities present. Such reconsiderations may allow us "to locate the ethical self as a locus of resistance to the systematicity of knowledge-power processes; a locus of resistance which operates in ways which enable the interstices in those systems to be exploited and the reproduction of control to be traversed or subverted" (Chesters, 2007, p. 245).

> E te Manu Ariki Whakatakapōkai, te Manu Tute
> Te Manu Tū Rae, Rere atu, Rere mai
>
> *Likening the majestic steadfast leadership of migratory birds to the bilingual/ immersion educational alternative of Kōhanga Reo, it is through this system which our tamariki/mokopuna (children and grandchildren) are nurtured and will take flight in whatever direction they wish*

References

Aitken, H., Piggot-Irvine, E., Bruce Ferguson, P., McGrath, F., & Ritchie, J. (2008). *Learning to Teach: Success Case Studies of Teacher Induction in Aotearoa New Zealand*. Wellingotn: New Zealand Teachers Council.

Ballara, A. (1986). *Proud to Be White? A Survey of Pakeha Prejudice in New Zealand*. Auckland: Heinemann.

Chesters, G. (2007). Complex and minor: Deleuze and the alterglobalization movement(s). In A. Hickey-Moody & P. Malins (Eds), *Deleuzian Encounters: Studies in Contemporary Social Issues* (pp. 236–250). Houndmills, Basingstoke, Hampshire, and New York: Palgrave Macmillan.

Dixon, R., Widdowson, D., Meagher-Lundberg, P., McMurchy-Pilkington, A., & McMurchy-Pilkington, C. (2007). *Evaluation of Promoting Early Childhood Education (ECE) Participation Project*. Report to the Ministry of Education. Wellington: Ministry of Education.

Ministry of Education. (2012a). *Education counts. Māori in ECE*. Wellington: Ministry of Education. Retrieved from http://www.educationcounts.govt.nz/statistics/ece2/mori-in-ece.

Ministry of Education. (2012b). *Me Kōrero. Let's Talk. Ka hikitia. Accelerating success 2103–2107*. Wellington: Ministry of Education. Retrieved from http://www.minedu.govt.nz/~/media/MinEdu/Files/TheMinistry/KaHikitia/English/MeKoreroLetsTalk.pdf.

New Zealand Ministry of Education. (1996). *Te Whāriki. He whāriki mātauranga mō ngā mokopuna o Aotearoa: Early childhood curriculum*. Wellington: Learning Media. Retrieved from http://www.educate.ece.govt.nz/~/media/Educate/Files/Reference%20Downloads/whariki.pdf.

New Zealand Ministry of Education. (2011). *Briefing to the Incoming Minister*. Wellington: Ministry of Education. Retrieved from http://www.minedu.govt.nz/~/media/MinEdu/Files/TheMinistry/PolicyAndStrategy/EducationBIM2011.pdf.

New Zealand Ministry of Education. (2013). *Ka hikitia. Accelerating success. 2013–2017. The Māori education strategy*. Wellington, New Zealand: Ministry of Education. Retrieved from http://www.minedu.govt.nz/theMinistry/PolicyAndStrategy/KaHikitia.aspx.

Piggot-Irvine, E., Aitken, H., Ritchie, J., Bruce Ferguson, P., & McGrath, F. (2009). Induction of newly qualified teachers in New Zealand. *Asia-Pacific Journal of Teacher Education, 37*(2), 175–198.

Robertson, J., Gunn, T. R., Lanumata, T., & Pryor, J. (2007). *Parental Decision Making in Relation to the Use of Early Childhood Education Services*. Report to the Ministry of Education. Wellington: Ministry of Education.

Rushkoff, D. (2013). *Present Shock: When Everything Happens Now*. USA: Current Hardcover.

Skerrett, M. E.(2011). *Whakamanahia te reo Māori: He tirohanga rangahau*. A review of the literature with relevance for te reo Māori competence of graduates from Māori medium initial teacher education programs. Wellington, NZ: New Zealand Teachers Council. 232.

Statistics New Zealand. Tatauranga Aotearoa. (2010). *The social report. Te pūrongo oranga tangata. Cultural Identity*. Wellington: Statistics New Zealand. Retrieved from http://www.socialreport.msd.govt.nz/documents/cultural-identity-social-report-2010.pdf.

United Nations. (2007). *United Nations Declaration on the Rights of Indigenous Peoples*. A/RES/61/295: General Assembly. Retrieved from www.un.org/esa/socdev/unpfii/documents/DRIPS_en.pdf

Waitangi Tribunal. (2010). *Te Reo Māori. Wai 262*. Pre publication report. Wellington: Waitangi Tribunal. Retrieved from http://www.waitangitribunal.govt.nz/scripts/reports/reports/262/056831F7-3388-45B5-B553-A37B8084D018.pdf.

Index

Accelerating Success 2013–2017, 47
additive, strong bilingual programs, 36
Ako – a two-way teaching and learning process, 48
Anglo settler, 78
anti-Māori racism, 29
Articles of Te Tiriti o Waitangi, 3, 38
assemblage, 4, 5, 95, 100, 113, 115, 116, 125
assimilatory policies, 69, 73

Ballara, Angela, 19, 21, 24, 25, 26, 27, 42, 53, 76, 87, 133, 137
becoming-ness, 116
Beeby, Clarence, 42, 53, 77, 87
Before Five (policy document), 6, 44, 45, 86, 88, 95, 108
Belich, James, 2, 3, 6, 7, 75, 77, 78, 87
belief systems, 3, 76, 78, 98
Belonging/Mana Whenua, 98
Bevan-Smith, John, 11, 21
bicultural, 5, 6, 57, 59, 61, 73, 92, 94, 97, 98, 101, 103, 105, 111, 114, 117, 118, 122, 128, 129
bilingual education, 36, 59, 62, 97
bilingual immersion settings, 36, 46, 61

bilingual/bicultural advancement, 5
bilingual/immersion, 35, 36, 43, 46, 47, 51, 56, 57, 59, 62, 132, 136
bilingualism, 10, 36, 59, 61, 134
binaries, 14
British colonization, 5
British colony, 74
British Commonwealth, 74
Busby, James, 3, 38

Cannella, Gaile, 10, 30
Carr, Margaret, 93, 101, 118, 127
categorisation, 47
civil rights, 81
cognitive dissonance, 13, 19
colonial courts, 51
colonial institutions, 11
colonial power, 12
colonization, 2, 4, 5, 40, 51, 68, 69, 73, 74, 75, 76, 77, 78, 81, 93, 97, 102, 105, 113, 117, 118, 125, 131
colour bar, 27
common law, 8, 37, 39
Communication/Mana Reo, 98
community, 47, 48, 65, 67, 77, 81, 86, 93, 102, 104, 108, 119, 122
conscientise, 135
constructivism, 6
Contribution/Mana Tangata, 98
core curriculum, 5, 42, 49, 69, 134

corporatisation, 94
counter colonial praxis, 10
counter-colonial discourses, 5, 69
Crown, 3, 37, 38, 40, 41, 42, 48, 49, 50, 52, 56, 58, 60, 69, 78, 93, 106, 114, 131
Cullen, Joy, 98, 99, 107, 108
cultural annihilation, 19
cultural archive, 52, 69
cultural bomb, 19
cultural deprivation, 80, 81
cultural diversity, 84
cultural schizophrenia, 19
cultural workers, 105, 108, 115, 122, 127
culturally rejuvenated iwi Māori, 43
culture shock, 5
curriculum reforms, 95
customary law, 20, 22
customs, 114

Davies, 11, 14, 16
Davies & Gannon, 11
Declaration of Independence
  1835 Declaration of Maori sovereignty, 3, 5, 37, 38, 55, 75, 131
deficit discourses, 73
deficit, theorising, 73, 80, 81, 82, 84, 88, 105, 132
dehegemonize
  settler historiographies, 11
dehegemonized, 5
Deleuze & Guattari, 4, 10, 13, 95, 100, 115, 116, 125
Deleuze, Gilles, 4, 7, 88, 95, 100, 107, 113, 115, 116, 125, 126, 127, 129, 136, 137
Deleuzeguattarian, 17, 29
Deleuzian-inspired, 74
deregulation, 64, 94
Desirable Objectives and Practices (DOPs), 100, 101, 109
desirings, 115, 116
deterritorialization, 4, 10, 134
deterritorializing, 29
developmental psychology, 6
devolution, 43, 94

discourse analysis, 10, 11, 18, 19, 31
discourses, 2, 4, 37, 42, 43, 58, 63, 66, 67, 74, 75, 81, 93, 97, 117, 120
discrimination, 18, 78
discursive power, 18
disenfranchisement, 74
dominant discourses, 52, 69
dominion over land, 39, 41
duplicitous, 39, 41

Early Childhood Care and Education (ECCE) service, 73, 74, 78, 81, 94, 97, 99, 102, 104, 105, 134, 135, 136
Early Childhood Education (ECE), 37, 44, 45, 46, 47, 50, 52, 58, 59, 60, 63, 96, 102, 107, 109, 126, 137
early years language nests, 35
Education Review Office (ERO), 12, 29, 50, 60, 61, 104, 105, 106, 107
egalitarianism, 74, 77, 84, 95, 97
empire, 74
Empowerment/Whakamana, 98
enforced assimilation, 51
English text
  Treaty of Waitangi, 38, 61
English-medium, 47
entrepreneurial, 65, 75
epistemology, 6, 114
ethical relationality, 74
ethical visions, 74, 75
Eugenicist race ideologies, 81
Eurocentric, 25
Eurocentrism, 10, 25, 30
exploit, 133
Exploration/Mana Aotūroa, 98

false consciousness, 27, 30
Family and Community/Whānau Tangata, 98
Fanon, Frantz, 11
Fishman, Joshua, 40, 53
five strands of the curriculum, 98
flaxroots movements, 6, 37, 74, 78, 95
  Kōhanga Reo Māori immersion language nests, 37
foreign system, 51

Index 141

Foucault, Michel, 4, 7, 18, 96, 113, 115, 126, 127
free-play, 79, 82
Freire, Paulo, 5, 7, 10, 64, 70, 105, 108, 113, 115, 127
Froebellian influences, 77
Fukushima disaster, 96
funding, 44, 45, 46, 47, 56, 57, 58, 60, 63, 103, 126, 132

global imperialism/capitalism, 74
global wealth, 74
globalization, 12, 95
Gordon, Lewis R., 11, 28, 29, 30
governance, 3, 38, 47
government expenditure, 50
governmentality, 96, 115
Guattari, Felix, 4, 7, 100, 107, 113, 115, 116, 126

hāngi (feast cooked in an earth oven), 82
hegemony, 37, 43, 46, 97
Hei Ara Kōkiri Tūwharetoa Education Initiative, 117, 118
Hērangi, Te Puea, 78
historiographies, 4, 41, 131
history, 5, 53, 74, 83, 88, 89, 105
Holistic Development/Kotahitanga, 98
homogenizing, 12, 27
hope, 5, 37, 66, 69, 74, 75
human rights, 2, 42, 75, 85
Hunn Report, 80

identity, 7, 38, 43, 47, 48, 82, 93, 96, 103, 104, 105, 108, 114, 120, 124, 134, 138
identity, language and culture, 47, 48, 103
ideology, 44, 65, 73
immanent practice, 74
imperialism, 12, 42, 68
inclusion/exclusion, 74
indigeneity, 97
Indigenous values, 96
Indigenous young children, 2
individualism, 6, 44, 85, 96, 136

influenza epidemics, 78
institutionalized racism, 11
integration, 6, 80, 97, 98, 114
intergenerational, 35, 40, 81, 99, 134
international imperialism, 74
invasion, 51
IQ tests, 81
iwi-Māori
    tribal groupings, 45, 49

Jordan, Barbara, 99, 108
juggernaut, 75

Ka Hikitia (policy document), 47, 49, 50, 54, 57, 69, 71, 103, 110, 134, 135
Ka tangi te tītī, ka tangi te kākā, ka tangi hoki ahau, 13
kai (ingested [generally food] for wellbeing), 81, 82, 92
kaiako (teachers), 121, 122
kaitiakitanga (active guardianship, stewardship, care-taking), 15, 125, 136
karakia (acknowledgement to the creator), 81, 124
kaupapa Māori, 6, 69, 97, 98, 106, 107, 113, 116, 124, 136
Kaupapa Māori Competencies for Teachers, 103
kawanatanga, 3, 37, 38, 131
Kawharu, Hugh, 38, 53
Kei Tua o te Pae (Assessment for learning: Early Childhood Exemplars), 103, 109
Key, John, 22, 23, 24
killer colonial languages, 17
kindergarten, 52, 118, 119, 122, 123, 124
King, Michael, 37, 38, 39, 75, 88
kingitanga (Māori king movement), 2, 20, 37, 38
'kiwi' culture and identity, 49
kiwi-feathered cloak, 35, 52, 134
Kōhanga Reo, 5, 8, 37, 43, 44, 45, 46, 50, 51, 52, 56, 58, 59, 60, 63, 68, 69, 98, 115, 131, 134, 136

land alienation, 5, 51
land confiscations, 39
Land Wars, 20
Lands Case, 40, 41, 52
Law of Contra Proferentem, 39
learners, 4, 49, 50, 60, 88, 103, 104, 105, 118, 119, 134
legitimate, 3, 45, 75
Lessa, Iara, 18
lines of flight, 74, 113, 116, 120, 125
linguafaction, 5, 10, 17, 19, 30, 40, 47, 50, 63, 131, 134

mahinga kai, 15, 16
Mahuta, Sir Robert, 82, 124
majoritarianism, 6
mana (prestige, value, authority, control, power, influence, status, spiritual power, charisma), 2, 3, 37, 38, 39, 52, 56, 78, 97, 117, 122, 133
manaakitanga (mana enhancing practices), 15, 81, 113, 117, 136
managerialist languaging, 102
Māori activism, 41, 84, 95
Māori Affairs, 45, 80, 84
Māori authority, 78
Māori bilingual/immersion, 37, 47, 56
Māori childrearing, 82, 93
Māori collectivism, 76
Māori Education Foundation, 80
Māori immersion, 2, 36, 37, 56, 58, 61, 63, 98
Māori independence, 76, 97
Māori language
  in education, 48, 49, 54, 71
  proficiency, 48, 57
Māori Language Act, 41, 42, 51, 53, 61, 70
Māori language education, 10, 19
Māori leadership, 3, 54, 71, 81
Māori medium, 5, 35, 46, 50, 59, 62, 69, 97, 138
Māori political movement, 78
Māori potential approach, 48
Māori preschools, 6
Māori rights, 39, 51, 76

Māori text
  Te Tiriti o Waitangi, 37, 38, 39, 61, 97, 98
Māori Women's Welfare League, 80
Māori/English bilingual speakers (MEBS), 59
marae, 16, 30, 31
marae (traditional Māori gathering places), 48, 80, 81, 82
marginalisation, 74, 83
market fundamentalism, 95
marketable commodity, 96
marketisation, 44
May, Helen, 36, 53, 74, 77, 78, 79, 84, 86, 88, 89, 93, 98, 99, 101, 108, 119, 125, 127
McDonald, Geraldine, 80, 81, 89
Meade Report, 44, 45
Metge, Joan, 80, 83, 89
Mikaere, Ani, 42, 54
Minister of Native Affairs, 78
missionaries, 39, 75, 78
monolingual English, 46, 62, 131
multicultural education, 59, 84
Mutu, Margaret, 37, 39, 42, 54
myth making, 52, 69
mythological, 97, 133
mythological discourses, 18
mythopoeia
  process of creating myths, 22

narratives, 6, 69, 99, 117, 133, 134
National Advisory Committee on Māori Education (NACME), 83
negative stereotyping, 81
neo-conservative ideologies, 101
neoliberalism, 6, 43, 57, 62, 63, 64, 65, 69, 70, 94, 95, 96, 109, 110, 133, 136
neoliberalist, 6, 95
New Right, 44
New Zealand Teachers Council (professional body overseeing teacher education and registration), 103, 104, 106, 107, 110, 137, 138

Index 143

Ngā Arohaehae Whai Hua (self-review guidelines), 102, 109
Ngāi Tahu, 15, 16, 49
Ngata, Sir Apirana, 78, 79
non-compulsory, 36, 95

'official' language of New Zealand the Māori language, 42
ontological, 45
Orange, Claudia, 3, 7, 20, 75, 76, 90, 93, 110
Organisation for Economic Co-operation and Development (OECD), 95
Otago settlement, 15

Pacific islands, 74, 75, 96, 102, 115
Pākehā, 40, 43, 45, 75, 79, 80, 83, 84, 93, 98, 99, 106, 113, 118, 122, 135
Papatūānuku (Earth Mother), 15, 17 115
Parata, Wi, 40
parental engagement, 45, 46
parent-led, as defined in policy, 46, 57, 58, 63, 115
participation policy, 45
partnership, 41, 48, 50, 52, 60, 63, 93, 100, 101, 102
Pathways to the Future (policy document), 35, 45, 46, 57, 58, 102, 109
patriarchal hierarchies, 29
pedagogy, 6, 56, 57, 63, 65, 66, 67, 69, 70, 87, 106, 108, 110, 111, 112, 113, 124, 125, 126
people's movement, 45
planning, implementation and evaluation, 46
Playcentre, 52, 79, 80, 84, 115
policy divide, 46
political developments, 45, 51
Pomare, Sir Maui, 78
population census, 135
power hierarchies, 10, 30
pōwhiri (welcoming ceremony), 81
praxis, 5, 6, 66, 105, 122, 128

preamble
 Treaty of Waitangi, 38
presentism, 133
primary/elementary schooling, 36, 46, 47, 48, 50, 62, 74, 77, 82, 88, 135, 136
priority learners, 43, 86
privatization, 6, 94, 96, 115, 23, 27
problematic partnership, 52
productive partnerships, 48
professional development, 48, 61
professionalization, 47
professionally educated teachers, 46
progressive traditions, 77
Promoting Participation Project (Ministry of Education Project), 45
proprietary rights
 Māori, 40
Proud to be white? A Survey of Pākehā Prejudice in New Zealand, 19
public good, 27

quality, 36, 43, 44, 45, 46, 47, 48, 49, 57, 58, 63, 86, 100, 101, 102, 105, 109, 125, 134, 135
The quality journey. He haerenga whai hua, 101
The quality journey. He haerenga whai hua, 109
Quality in Action. Te Mahi Whai hua, 101

R v Symonds, 20, 22, 39, 106
race
 concept of, 11, 20
racism, 3, 13, 23, 28, 29, 31, 41, 78, 84, 97
racist, 131
racist colonial thinking, 131
Rangatira (sovereign chiefs), 37
Ratana, Wiremu Tahupotiki, 77
Rau, Cheryl, 2, 98, 111, 113, 116, 117, 118, 119, 120, 123, 124, 125, 126, 128, 129, 135
reciprocal relationships, 6
Reedy, Tamati and Tilly, 93
regulatory framework, 43, 44, 57, 62
Relationships/Ngā Hononga, 98

renarrativization, 5, 69
resistance, 12, 13, 20, 27
resources, 41, 47, 57, 62, 63, 69, 74, 78, 114, 132
reterritorializing, 29, 97, 125
revernacularization, 5, 43, 56, 132
rhizomatic mutiplicities, 115
risk management, 96
Ritchie, Jane, 82
The Royal Society of New Zealand, 50, 55, 61, 71
rural/urban separation, 79
rush of reform, 44

Salmond, Anne, 75, 90, 93, 112
savage, 21, 22, 29, 30
savages, 40
second language acquisition, 48
secondary/high school, 36, 47, 48, 50, 135, 136
secular and compulsory education, 42
settlerism, 3, 5
settlers, 3, 6, 40, 41, 75, 76, 78
Simon, Judith, 81, 84, 90, 93, 106, 112
Smith, Graham, 84
Smith, Linda, 12,42, 53, 54, 68, 86, 91, 93, 112, 116, 123, 126, 129
social and economic policy, 6
Social Darwinist, 81
social justice, 6, 65, 67, 95, 97
sociocultural, 2, 6, 92, 98, 100, 114
sociocultural dislocation, 30, 51
socioeconomic status, 74
sociolinguistics, 10, 43
sovereign power, 3, 38
sovereignty, 37, 38, 39, 75, 76, 78
Stewart-Harawira, Makere, 12, 27, 41, 54
story-telling, 67, 68, 133
strategic plan, 45, 54, 71, 102
striated space, 14, 116
striations, 14, 17, 95
structural level, 47
struggle, 13, 19, 31
subjugated
    indigenous knowledges, 12

subjugation, 21, 39
subtractive assimilatory programs, 36, 69
success, 5, 47, 48, 49, 52, 54, 59, 69, 71, 80, 110, 119, 137

Tagata Pasefika, 115
Taha Māori (Māori dimension), 84
taha wairua (spiritual wellbeing), 101
Tainui tribe, 78
tamariki (children), 6, 66, 68, 83, 101, 104, 118, 122, 124, 129, 136
Tangata Tiriti (people who now live in Aotearoa by virtue of the Treaty), 5
Tangata Whenua (people of the land, Indigenous people, Māori), 5, 12, 17, 30, 98, 100, 101, 115
tangihanga (ways of burying the dead), 82, 85, 106
taonga, 42, 49, 51, 52, 76, 79
Taonui, Aperahama, 35, 52
Tātaiako: Cultural Competencies for Teachers of Māori Learners, 103, 104, 110, 136
Tau Mai Te Reo (policy document), 47, 49, 50
Taylor, Henry, 76, 77
Tāwhiwhirangi, Dame Iritana, 51, 52
te ao Māori (Māori world views, language and values), 6, 70, 73, 77, 98, 99, 101, 103, 105, 106, 120, 122, 135, 136
Te Kōhanga Reo (TKR), 2, 35, 43, 44, 45, 46, 47, 50, 56, 58, 60, 63, 69, 93
Te Kooti Rikirangi, 40
Te Rangi Hiroa, 4, 8
Te Rangihau, John, 45
te reo Māori (the Māori language), 4, 5, 41, 42, 43, 44, 51, 57, 60, 61, 69, 78, 81, 86, 117, 132, 133, 134, 135, 138
Te Tiriti o Waitangi, 3, 5, 6, 35, 37, 38, 41, 74, 75, 76, 78, 79, 83, 93, 97, 100, 101, 102, 106, 111, 114, 118, 119, 128, 135

Te Whāriki (NZ early childhood curriculum), 2, 5, 6, 49, 54, 59, 60, 61, 70, 73, 75, 79, 89, 92, 93, 95, 97, 98, 99, 100, 101, 102, 103, 105, 106, 107, 108, 109, 110, 111, 112, 113, 114, 115, 118, 119, 125, 126, 127, 128, 134, 135, 137
Te Whatu Pōkeka (Assessment of Māori children), 103, 110, 127
teacher credentials, 46
teacher education, 6, 46, 47, 49, 57, 83, 84, 105, 132, 135, 138
teacher recruitment, 48
teacher-led, as defined in policy, 46, 57, 58, 60, 63, 115
technologies, 115, 133
terralinguistics, 14
territorialization, 4, 5, 10, 13, 14, 15, 16, 17, 18, 20, 30, 132
territorialized, 14, 16, 17, 29, 30
The Dominion Post, 19, 23, 25, 26, 28, 30
tikanga, 39, 44, 81, 86, 98, 105, 118
tino rangatiratanga, 3, 68, 97
Titiro Whakamuri, Hoki Whakamua, 124, 128
tokenistic gesture, 134
traditional lands, 39
transformative, 10
Treaty of Waitangi, 2, 6, 7, 10, 20, 22, 27, 37, 40, 47, 54, 74, 75, 86, 90, 93, 95, 110
Treaty/Tiriti breaches, 4, 5, 57, 60
tribal dialects, 106
Tuck, Eve, 19, 28
tūrangawaewae (place to stand), 52

unfoldings, 113, 116, 123, 125
United Nations Declaration on the Rights of Indigenous Peoples, 132, 138
USA Headstart, 82
utu (current context, reciprocity), 136

vernacular, 51
visionary leadership, 74

wairuatanga (spiritual interconnectedness), 113, 117, 125
Waitangi Tribunal, 4, 5, 8, 37, 41, 42, 43, 45, 50, 51, 52, 55, 56, 57, 58, 59, 60, 61, 62, 68, 71, 84, 85, 91, 93, 112, 132, 134, 138
Waite, Jeffrey, 50, 55, 61, 71
Walker, Ranginui, 2, 3, 8, 29, 75, 76, 78, 80, 83, 84, 91, 93, 112
Well-Being/Mana Atua, 98, 103
Western capitalism, 41
whakapapa (Māori ancestry), 81, 117, 121
whānau/family, 2, 6
whanaungatanga (relationships), 113, 117, 122, 136
wharenui (Māori meeting house), 121, 122
whitestream, 35, 42, 44, 46, 47, 51, 58, 60, 61, 69, 73, 92, 93, 103, 106, 118, 134
Wi Parata, 40

GPSR Compliance

The European Union's (EU) General Product Safety Regulation (GPSR) is a set of rules that requires consumer products to be safe and our obligations to ensure this.

If you have any concerns about our products, you can contact us on

ProductSafety@springernature.com

In case Publisher is established outside the EU, the EU authorized representative is:

Springer Nature Customer Service Center GmbH
Europaplatz 3
69115 Heidelberg, Germany

www.ingramcontent.com/pod-product-compliance
Lightning Source LLC
LaVergne TN
LVHW041955060526
838200LV00002B/29